The post-war German tradition

Kempe Keilberth Sawallisch
Kubelik Cluytens

Discographies compiled
by John Hunt

CONTENTS

- 3   Acknowledgement
- 5   Introduction
- 7   Rudolf Kempe
- 49   Joseph Keilberth
- 87   Wolfgang Sawallisch
- 138   Wolfgang Sawallisch as pianist
- 145   Rafael Kubelik
- 199   André Cluytens
- 239   Credits

Published 1996 by John Hunt

Designed by Richard Chlupaty

Copyright 1996 John Hunt

The Post-War German Tradition
Published by John Hunt.
Designed by Richard Chluparty
© 1996 John Hunt
reprinted 2009
ISBN 978-0-952582-72-4

Sole distributors:
Travis & Emery,
17 Cecil Court,
London, WC2N 4EZ,
United Kingdom.
(+44) 20 7 459 2129.
sales@travis-and-emery.com

ACKNOWLEDGEMENT

This publication has been made possible by generous support from the following

Richard Ames, New Barnet
Stefano Angeloni, Italy
Yoshihiro Asada, Japan
Jack Atkinson, Tasmania
Gary Bagnall, Co. Antrim
Javier Casellas, Barcelona
J. Charrington, Cardiff
Edward Chibas, Caracas
F. De Vilder, Bussum
John Derry, Newcastle-upon-Tyne
Erik Dervos, London
J. Dietz, Gateshead
Christopher Dowling, London
Peter Ebner, Milan
Shuntaro Enatsu, Japan
Bill Flowers, London
Henry Fogel, Chicago
Gerhard Frenzel, Celle
Peter Fu, Hong Kong
Nobuo Fukumoto, Japan
Peter Fulop, Toronto
James Giles, Sidcup
Jean-Pierre Goossens, Luxemburg
Gordon Grant, Seattle
Johann Gratz, Vienna
Peter Hamann, Bochum
Michael Harris, London
Tadashi Hasegawa, Japan
Naoya Hirabayashi, Japan
Donald Hodgman, New York
Martin Holland, Sale
John Hughes, Brisbane
Richard Igler, Vienna
Shiro Kawai, Japan
Masahito Kawashima, Japan
Koji Kinoshima, Japan
Detlef Kissmann, Solingen

Eric Kobe, Lucerne
Jean-Fr. Longerstay, Brussels
Ernst Lumpe, Soest
John Mallinson, Hurst Green
Carlo Marinelli, Rome
Kevork Marouchian, Munich
John Meriton, Manchester
Philip Moores, Stafford
Bruce Morrison, Gillingham
W. Moyle, Ombersley
Alan Newcombe, Hamburg
Takaaki Omoto, Japan
Gregory Page-Turner, Bridport
Hugh Palmer, Chelmsford
James Pearson, Vienna
Sergi Petit, Barcelona
Donald Priddon, London
Patrick Russell, Calstock
Yves Saillard, Mollie-Margot
Robin Scott, Bradford
R. Simmons, Pewsey
Roger Smithson, London
Göran Söderwall, Stockholm
T. Spoors, Newcastle-upon-Tyne
Holger Steinhauff, Stemwede
Neville Sumpter, Northolt
Yoshihiro Suzuki, Japan
Swiss Sound Archive, Lugano
Masashi Takenata, Japan
H.A. Van Dijk, Apeldoorn
Mario Vicentini, Italy
Hiromitsu Wada, Japan
Malcolm Walker, Harrow
Urs Weber, St. Gallen
Nigel Wood, London
G. Wright, Romford
Ken Wyman, Brentwood
Michiaki Yabuta, Japan

Saturday, 31st May, 1958

The 35th performance at the Royal Opera House
of

ELEKTRA

Tragedy in one act by Hugo von Hofmannsthal

Music by Richard Strauss

Scenery and costumes by Isabel Lambert

CONDUCTOR - RUDOLF KEMPE

THE COVENT GARDEN OPERA CHORUS
Chorus Master - Douglas Robinson

THE COVENT GARDEN ORCHESTRA
Leader - Charles Taylor

RICHARD STRAUSS, 1864-1949

This opera was first produced at Dresden on 25th January, 1909 with Annie Krull, Schumann-Heink, Margarete Siems and Karl Perron, conductor Ernst von Schuch. It was first performed in London, in German, at the Royal Opera House, Covent Garden, on the 19th February, 1910 with Edyth Walker, von Mildenburg, Frances Rose, and Hermann Weidemann, conductor Thomas Beecham; the first performance in English was at Hull, on 28th February, 1912. The opera was revived at Covent Garden in 1925 with Gertrud Kappel and Maria Olczewska, conductor Karl Alwin and in 1938 with Rose Pauly and Kerstin Thorborg, conductor Sir Thomas Beecham. The first performances after the war in this theatre were in May 1953 with Erna Schluter Annelies Kupper, Edith Coates, Hans Braun, conductor Erich Kleiber.

CHARACTERS IN ORDER OF APPEARANCE

Five Maids	LAURIS ELMS
	NOREEN BERRY
	JOSEPHINE VEASEY
	MARIE COLLIER
	JEANNETTE SINCLAIR
The Overseer	JUNE GRANT
Elektra	GERDA LAMMERS
Chrysothemis, her sister	HEDWIG MULLER-BUTOW
Klytemnestra, their mother	GEORGINE VON MILINKOVIC
The Confidante	PHYLLIS SIMONS
Trainbearer	PATRICIA DU HEAUME
A Young Servant	DERMOT TROY
An Old Servant	CHARLES MORRIS
Orest, brother of Elektra and Chrysothemis	OTAKAR KRAUS
Orest's Tutor	DAVID KELLY
Aegisth	EDGAR EVANS

Servants of the Household

THE POST-WAR GERMAN TRADITION

When one talks about the great German tradition of conductors, names which spring to mind are Richter, Nikisch, Weingartner, Furtwängler, Walter, Erich Kleiber and Krauss - and more recently Carlos Kleiber and Karajan. Figures such as these, who in today's jargon would probably be called superstars, were supported by a vast array of **Kapellmeister**, less exalted perhaps but craftsmen of the highest order. Long apprentice years in provincial and municipal opera houses had equipped these men with an expertise almost unattainable in today's musical world (talent and good public relations are all that is talked about now). Where would we have been in the 1950s and 1960s without the talents of the like of Knappertsbusch, Böhm, Jochum, Krips and Schuricht, to name but a few?

Yet already in the 1950s there was talk of the **Kapellmeister** being a dying breed. The tradition was in fact still being upheld by a few, some of whose careers were only just beginning and others whose work had its beginnings before or during World War II. Long periods of hard work, sometimes in the orchestral ranks or as repetiteurs behind the scenes, meant that when it came to making records they knew a thing or two about balances, about the relating of soloists - vocal or instrumental - to an orchestra.

When we think of a conductor inspiring his players, it need not necessarily be in a flamboyant or extrovert way: more a case, perhaps, of motivating and unifying that diverse group of men known as the orchestra. Such were the methods of **Rudolf Kempe** (his apprentice years had begun in the ranks of the Leipzig Gewandhaus Orchestra) and **Joseph Keilberth** (building up a notable orchestra from scratch in German-occupied Prague).

Similar credentials are found to be held by **Wolfgang Sawallisch**, who during his association with Munich's Bayerische Staatsoper from 1954 (from 1971 as Generalmusikdirektor) until 1992 conducted around 1400 performances of at least 48 full-length stage works. In his discography, a separate section is also devoted to his work as a major piano accompanist to Lieder singers.

Two "outsiders" have also shown a deep spiritual affinity with German music: the Czech **Rafael Kubelik**, who spent many fruitful years with the Bavarian Radio Orchestra after having held significant musical directorships both in Europe and America; and **André Cluytens**, who for all his upbringing in French-speaking centres and a resultant command of French opera, yet demonstrated a strong attachment to German symphonic and operatic music, repeatedly returning to the Bayreuth Festival as a guest conductor.

John Hunt

Rudolf Kempe
1910-1976

With valuable assistance from Malcolm Walker

Discography compiled
by John Hunt

Drawing of Rudolf Kempe by Brian Pinder

JOHANN SEBASTIAN BACH (1685-1750)

Orchestral Suite No 3

Berlin November- December 1957	BPO	LP: Electrola E 80018/WCLP 539 CD: EMI CDZ 252 2332

Concerto for 4 pianos BWV 1065

Munich 1972	Bavarian RO Kempe, 1st piano Rieger & Sawallisch, 3rd and 4th pianos, Kubelik, conducting from 2nd piano	CD: Hunt CDMP 4941

JOSEF BAYER (1852-1913)

Die Puppenfee, ballet music

Vienna December 1960	VPO	LP: HMV ALP 1974/ASD 525 LP: EMI XLP 30083/SXLP 30083

LUDWIG VAN BEETHOVEN (1770-1827)

Symphony No 1

Munich June 1972	Munich PO	LP: EMI SLS 892/1C 147 02606-02513Q LP: Angel 6093 LP: EMI CFP 4406 CD: EMI CES 568 5182

Symphony No 2

Munich December 1972- April 1973	Munich PO	LP: EMI SLS 892/1C 147 02506-02513Q LP: Angel 6093 LP: EMI CFP 4406

Symphony No 3 "Eroica"

Berlin September 1959	BPO	LP: HMV ALP 1854/ASD 426 LP: Electrola E 80535/STE 80535/SMVP 8004 LP: Capitol L 9218/SL 9218 LP: World Records T 942/ST 942 LP: EMI 1C 047 50507 CD: EMI CDZ 762 6232/CES 568 5182 <u>CDZ 762 6232 incorrectly dated 1972</u>
Munich June 1972	Munich PO	LP: EMI SLS 892/1C 147 02506-02513Q LP: Angel 6093 LP: EMI 1C 051 02507/CFP 41 44101

<u>An HMV version of the Eroica was planned with the Philharmonia Orchestra for June 1956 but the recording sessions did not take place</u>

Symphony No 4

Munich April 1973	Munich PO	LP: EMI SLS 892/1C 147 02506-02513Q LP: Angel 6093 LP: EMI 1C 037 02508/CFP 4407

Symphony No 5

Munich December 1971	Munich PO	LP: EMI SLS 892/1C 147 02506-02513Q LP: Angel 6093 LP: EMI 1C 051 02509/CFP 41 44151 CD: EMI CES 568 5182
Zürich 1972	Tonhalle-Orchester	LP: Tudor 73001 LP: Ex Libris EL 16605

Symphony No 6 "Pastoral"

Munich June 1972	Munich PO	LP: EMI SLS 892/1C 147 02506-02513Q LP: Angel 6093 LP: EMI ESD 7004/CFP 41 44191 CD: EMI CES 568 5192/CDCFP 4419

Symphony No 7

Dresden June 1970	Dresden Staatskapelle	LP: Orfeo S079 832I LP: Eterna 827 001 Rehearsal only
Munich June 1972	Munich PO	LP: EMI SLS 892/1C 147 02506-02513Q LP: Angel 6093 LP: EMI 1C 051 02511/CFP 4408

Another version of the 7th Symphony, in which Kempe conducts the Bamberg SO, was published in USA in cassette form, Encore EC 5005

Symphony No 8

Munich December 1972	Munich PO	LP: EMI SLS 892/1C 147 02506-02513Q LP: Angel 6093 LP: EMI 1C 125 02761-02762/CFP 41 44151 LP: EMI 1C 142 02761-02762 CD: EMI CES 568 5192
Date not confirmed	Bavarian RO	CD: Originals SH 809

Symphony No 9 "Choral"

Munich May-June 1973	Munich PO Munich Philharmonic and Motet Choirs Koszut, Fassbaender, Gedda, McIntyre	LP: EMI SLS 892/1C 147 02506-02513Q LP: Angel 6093 LP: EMI 1C 125 02761-02762/CFP 41 44181 LP: EMI 1C 142 02761-02762

Piano Concerto No 3

Turin April 1962	RAI Torino Orchestra Kempff	CD: Curcio-Hunt CON 35

Piano Concerto No 5 "Emperor"

Berlin June 1957- April 1958	BPO J.Gimpel	LP: Electrola E 80025/STE 80025 LP: EMI XLP 20004/SXLP 20004 LP: Genesis GS 1002
London 1964	RPO Firkusny	LP: Reader's Digest RD 4601 LP: RCA GL 25014 CD: Menuet 16 00152

Coriolan, Overture

Berlin September 1957	BPO	LP: HMV ALP 1663/ASD 336/MFP 2056 LP: Electrola E 80029/STE 80029 LP: EMI SMVP 8037/1C 047 50513 LP: Capitol G 7140/SG 7140/SP 8635

Fidelio, Overture

Berlin September 1957	BPO	LP: HMV ALP 1663/ASD 336/MFP 2056 LP: Electrola E 80029/STE 80029 LP: EMI SMVP 8037/1C 047 50513 LP: Capitol G 7140/SG 7140/SP 8635 CD: EMI CDZ 762 6232/CES 568 5182

Egmont, Overture

Berlin September 1957	BPO	LP: HMV ALP 1663/ASD 336/MFP 2056 LP: Electrola E 80029/STE 80029 LP: EMI SMVP 8037/1C 047 50513 LP: Capitol G 7140/SG 7140/SP 8635 CD: EMI CDZ 762 6232/CES 568 5182
Dresden June 1970	Dresden Staatskapelle	LP: Orfeo S079 832I LP: Eterna 827 001 Rehearsal only
Munich December 1971	Munich PO	LP: EMI SLS 892/1C 147 02506-02513Q LP: Angel 6093 LP: EMI CFP 4408/1C 051 02509

<u>Another version of Egmont Overture, recorded by Kempe with the Bamberg SO, was issued in cassette form in USA, Encore EC 5005</u>

Die Geschöpfe des Prometheus, Overture

Berlin   BPO
September 1957
- LP: HMV ALP 1663/ASD 336/MFP 2056
- LP: Electrola E 80029/STE 80029
- LP: EMI SMVP 8037/1C 047 50513
- LP: Capitol G 7140/SG 7140/SP 8635
- CD: EMI CDZ 762 6232/CES 568 5182

Munich   Munich PO
December 1971
- LP: EMI SLS 892/1C 147 02506-02513Q
- LP: Angel 6093
- LP: EMI CFP 41 44101/1C 051 02507

Leonore No 3, Overture

Berlin   BPO
July 1957
- LP: HMV ALP 1663/ASD 336/MFP 2056
- LP: Electrola E 80029/STE 80029
- LP: EMI SMVP 8037/1C 047 50513
- LP: Capitol G 7140/SG 7140/SP 8635

Munich   Munich PO
December 1971
- LP: EMI SLS 892/1C 147 02506-02513Q
- LP: Angel 6093
- LP: EMI CFP 4407/1C 037 02508

HECTOR BERLIOZ (1803-1869)

Symphonie fantastique

Berlin   BPO
March 1959
- LP: Electrola E 80491/STE 80491
- LP: EMI XLP 20088/SXLP 20088/1C 051 03013
- CD: EMI CES 568 5252

Le carnaval romain, Overture

Vienna   VPO
December 1958
- LP: HMV ALP 1765/ASD 330/SMVP 8061
- LP: EMI XLP 30077/SXLP 30077
- CD: EMI CES 568 5252
- CD: Toshiba Shinseido SGR 8008

GEORGES BIZET (1838-1875)

L'Arlésienne, Suites Nos 1 and 2

1963   Bamberg SO
- LP: Eurodisc 70795KK/88705XDK
- LP: Oriole RM 200/RM 52200

JOHANNES BRAHMS (1833-1897)

Symphony No 1

Berlin January 1959	BPO	LP: HMV ALP 1772/ASD 350 LP: Electrola E 80459/STE 80459 LP: Capitol G 7208/SG 7208 LP: EMI MFP 2012/1C 047 50538 CD: Pantheon 18428 CD: Testament SBT 3054
Munich May 1975	Munich PO	LP: BASF 20 223914 LP: BASF BAC 3083/JB 23033 CD: Acanta 44 20942

Symphony No 2

Berlin June 1955	BPO	LP: HMV ALP 1386/XLP 30043 LP: Electrola E 80004 CD: Testament SBT 3054
June 1963	Bamberg SO	LP: Eurodisc 70611KK/27641XAK LP: World Records T 424/ST 424
Munich December 1975	Munich PO	LP: BASF DC 22 3922/JB 23033 CD: Acanta 44 20942

Symphony No 3

Berlin January 1960	BPO	LP: HMV ALP 1824/ASD 406 LP: Electrola E 80582/STE 80582 LP: EMI XLP 30100/SXLP 30100 CD: Testament SBT 3054
Munich December 1975	Munich PO	LP: BASF 20 223930/JB 23033 CD: Acanta 44 20942

Symphony No 4

Berlin December 1956	BPO	LP: HMV ALP 1545 LP: Electrola E 80017 LP: Capitol G 7100 CD: Testament SBT 3054
London November 1960	RPO	LP: HMV ALP 1894/ASD 461/1C 047 50800 LP: World Records T 932/ST 932 CD: Pantheon 18428
Munich November 1974	Munich PO	LP: BASF 20 223949/BAC 3064/JB 23033 CD: Acanta 44 20942
London 1975	BBCSO	Unpublished radio broadcast

Piano Concerto No 1

Berlin April 1958	BPO J.Gimpel	LP: Electrola E 80427/STE 80427 LP: EMI XLP 20010/SXLP 20010 CD: Royal Classics ROY 6436 <u>Royal Classics incorrectly dated 1967</u>

Piano Concerto No 2

London September 1975	RPO Gelber	LP: EMI SXDW 3020/1C 063 12788 LP: Connoisseur CSQ 20088 CD: EMI CZS 762 8832

Violin Concerto

Berlin September 1957	BPO Menuhin	LP: HMV ALP 1568/ASD 264 LP: Electrola E 90017/STE 90017 LP: Capitol PAO 8410/SG 7173 LP: EMI SXLP 30186/SHZE 716 LP: Eterna 825 261 CD: EMI CDZ 762 6082/CMS 762 5362 CD: EMI CES 568 5262 CD: Royal ROY 6483

Haydn Variations

Berlin November 1956	BPO	LP: Electrola E 80018/WCLP 539 CD: Testament SBT 3054
September 1963	Bamberg SO	LP: Eurodisc 70471KK/27641XAK LP: Oriole RM 201/RM 52201 LP: World Records T 437/ST 437
Munich November 1975	Munich PO	LP: BASF 20 223930/JB 23033 CD: Acanta 44 20942

Tragic Overture

Berlin January 1960	BPO	LP: HMV ALP 1824/ASD 406 LP: Electrola E 80582/STE 80582 LP: EMI XLP 30100/SXLP 30100 CD: Testament SBT 3054

Ein deutsches Requiem

Berlin June 1955	BPO St Hedwig's Choir Grümmer, Fischer-Dieskau	LP: HMV ALP 1351-1352/XLP 30073-30074 LP: Electrola E 90003-90004 LP: EMI 1C 147 28550-28551 CD: EMI CDH 764 7052

Piano Trio in C op 87

Munich 1973	C.Kempe, violin Kiskalt, cello Kempe, piano	Unpublished radio broadcast

BENJAMIN BRITTEN (1913-1976)

Sinfonia da Requiem

Dresden January 1976	Dresden Staatskapelle	LP: Eterna 827 012 CD: Berlin Classics BC 10972

MAX BRUCH (1838-1920)

Violin Concerto No 1

London	RPO	LP: Decca SXL 6573/417 2701
May 1972	Chung	CD: Decca 421 4492
		<u>Second movement</u>
		CD: Decca 443 5852

Scottish Fantasy for violin and orchestra

London	RPO	LP: Decca SXL 6573
May 1972	Chung	CD: Decca 425 0352/443 3312

ANTON BRUCKNER (1824-1896)

Symphony No 4 "Romantic"

Munich January 1976	Munich PO	LP: BASF 92 27931/EB 22739
Date not confirmed	Munich PO	CD: Artists Live Recordings FED 066

Symphony No 5

Munich May 1975	Munich PO	LP: BASF 92 25267/HA 22526

Symphony No 8

Munich May 1972	Munich PO	Unpublished radio broadcast
Zürich 1973	Tonhalle-Orchester	LP: Tudor 74003-74004 LP: Ex Libris EL 16607
Date not confirmed	BBC SO	Unpublished radio broadcast

FREDERIC CHOPIN (1810-1849)

Piano Concerto No 2

London April 1966	RPO Cherkassky	LP: Reader's Digest RD 4414 CD: Menuet 16 00132

ANTONIN DVORAK (1841-1904)

Symphony No 8

Düsseldorf November 1972	Munich PO	LP: BASF 29 217701

Symphony No 9 "From the New World"

Berlin September 1957	BPO	LP: HMV ALP 1623/ASD 380 LP: Electrola E 80026/STE 80026 LP: EMI XLP 30110/SXLP 30110 LP: EMI SMVP 8015/1C 047 50508 CD: EMI CDZ 252 2322/Royal 6440
London May 1963	RPO	LP: Reader's Digest RD 4213 CD: Menuet 16 00142
Zürich 1972	Tonhalle-Orchester	LP: Tudor 73002 LP: Ex Libris EL 16606

Serenade for strings

Munich May 1968	Munich PO	LP: CBS 72711/78210/61811 CD: Sony SBK 46331

Scherzo capriccioso

Berlin July 1957	BPO	LP: Electrola E 80027/WCLP 548
London January 1961	RPO	LP: HMV ALP 1880/ASD 449 LP: Angel 60098 LP: EMI XLP 30110/SXLP 30110/SXLP 30125 CD: EMI CDCFP 4587

Rusalka: Excerpt (O silver moon)

Berlin July 1957	BPO Lindermeier <u>Sung in German</u>	LP: Electrola E 80027/WCLP 548

REINHOLD GLIERE (1875-1956)

Harp Concerto

Leipzig 1950	Leipzig PO Joff	LP: Urania 7164/57164

CHRISTOPH WILLIBALD GLUCK (1714-1787)

Ballet Suite, arranged by Mottl

Vienna December 1961	VPO	LP: HMV ALP 1910/ASD 478 LP: Electrola E 80732/STE 80732 LP: Angel 35746

JAKOV GOTOVAC

Ero der Schelm: Excerpt (Kolo)

Vienna December 1961	VPO	LP: HMV ALP 1930/ASD 494 LP: World Records T 763/ST 763 LP: Angel 35975

CHARLES GOUNOD (1818-1893)

Faust: Excerpt (Waltz)

Vienna December 1961	VPO	LP: HMV ALP 1974/ASD 525

EDVARD GRIEG (1843-1907)

Piano Concerto

Munich May 1968	Munich PO Freire	LP: CBS 72712/61697/31041

GEORGE FRIDERIC HANDEL (1685-1759)

Music for the Royal Fireworks

Bamberg May 1962	Bamberg SO	LP: Electrola E 70495/STE 70495 CD: EMI CDZ 252 2332

JOSEPH HAYDN (1732-1809)

Symphony No 93

Munich 1968	Munich PO	LP: Intercord 70109 LP: Da Camera Magna SM 91509

Symphony No 104 "London"

London June 1956	Philharmonia	LP: HMV ALP 1471/MFP 2082 LP: Electrola E 80454 LP: Capitol G 7150/SG 7150 CD: EMI CDZ 568 7362

Sinfonia concertante for wind

Munich December 1966	Bavarian RO Soloists	CD: Orfeo C267 921B

RICHARD HEUBERGER (1850-1914)

Der Opernball, Overture

Vienna January 1958	VPO	LP: HMV ALP 1637/ASD 279 LP: Electrola E 80455/STE 80455/ E 41142/STE 41142 LP: Capitol G 7167/SG 7167 LP: Angel 6109 LP: EMI XLP 30083/SXLP 30083

ENGELBERT HUMPERDINCK (1854-1921)

Hänsel und Gretel, Suite arranged by Kempe

London January 1961	RPO	LP: HMV ALP 1892/ASD 460 LP: Angel 60056 LP: World Records T 736/ST 736 CD: EMI CDZ 568 7362

LEOS JANACEK (1854-1928)

Sinfonietta

London August 1974	BBC SO	CD: BBC/IMP DMCD 98

Glagolithic Mass

London May 1973	RPO Brighton Festival Chorus Kubiak, Collins, Tear, Schöne	LP: Decca SXL 6600/411 7261

ARAM KHACHATURIAN (1903-1978)

Cello Concerto

Leipzig ca. 1952	Leipzig RO Posegga	LP: Urania 7119

ZOLTAN KODALY (1882-1967)

Hary Janos, Suite

Vienna December 1961	VPO	LP: HMV ALP 1930/ASD 494 LP: Electrola E 70511/STE 70511 LP: Angel 35975 LP: World Records T 763/ST 763

ERICH WOLFGANG KORNGOLD (1897-1957)

Symphony in F sharp

Munich November 1972	Munich PO	LP: RCA ARL1-0443/GL 42919 CD: Varèse-Sarabande VSD 5346

FRANZ LEHAR (1870-1948)

Gold und Silber, waltz

Vienna January 1958	VPO	LP: HMV ALP 1637/ASD 279 LP: EMI XLP 30060/SXLP 30060 LP: Capitol G 7167/SG 7167 LP: Angel 6109 LP: EMI 1C 151 01463-01464 CD: EMI CZS 568 7362
Dresden September 1972	Dresden Staatskapelle	LP: Eurodisc 86847IU LP: RCA LRL1-5044 LP: Eterna 845 105 CD: Berlin Classics BC 90752/90072

FRANZ LISZT (1811-1886)

Totentanz for piano and orchestra

Munich May 1968	Munich PO Freire	LP: CBS 72713

GUSTAV MAHLER (1860-1911)

Symphony No 1

London May 1965	BBC SO	Unpublished radio broadcast

Kindertotenlieder

Berlin June 1955	BPO Fischer-Dieskau	LP: HMV BLP 1081/XLP 30044 LP: Electrola E 70004/SME 91387 LP: Angel 60272 LP: EMI 1C 063 00898/100 8981 CD: EMI CDC 747 6572

PIETRO MASCAGNI (1863-1945)

L'Amico Fritz, Intermezzo

Vienna December 1961	VPO	LP: HMV ALP 1974/ASD 525

ENTE AUTONOMO

TEATRO ALLA SCALA

CONCERTI 1960

Venerdì 21 e sabato 22 ottobre - ore 21.15

TREDICESIMO CONCERTO

Direttore
RUDOLF KEMPE

Violoncellista
ENRICO MAINARDI

ORCHESTRA DELLA SCALA

PROGRAMMA

LUDWIG van BEETHOVEN — *LEONORA N. 3 - OUVERTURE*
(Bonn 1770 - Vienna 1827)

SERGEI S. PROKOFIEV — *SINFONIA N. 7*
(Sontsovka 1891 - Mosca 1953)
    Moderato
    Allegretto
    Andante espressivo
    Vivace   Prima esecuzione a Milano

ROBERT SCHUMANN — *CONCERTO IN LA MINORE PER VIOLONCELLO E ORCHESTRA*
(Zwickau 1810 - Endenich 1856)
    Allegro ma non troppo
    Adagio
    Molto vivace

PAUL HINDEMITH — *METAMORFOSI SINFONICHE SU TEMI DI WEBER*
(Hanau 1895)
    Allegro - Moderato - Vivace
    Andantino - Marcia

BAYERISCHE STAATSOPER
NATIONALTHEATER MÜNCHEN

Samstag, 19. Dezember 1970
Anläßlich des 200. Geburtstages des Komponisten

FIDELIO

Oper in zwei Aufzügen

Text nach dem Französischen von Treitschke

Musik von

LUDWIG VAN BEETHOVEN

Musikalische Leitung: Rudolf Kempe
Inszenierung: Rudolf Hartmann
Bühnenbild: Helmut Jürgens · Kostüme: Sophia Schröck

FELIX MENDELSSOHN-BARTHOLDY (1809-1847)

Symphony No 3 "Scotch"

Dresden 1951	Diresden Staatskapelle	78: Ultraphon 23953-23957 LP: Supraphon LKS 30017/LPV 213 LP: Supraphon LPM 11-12/E 10159 LP: Parliament PLP 142

The Hebrides, Overture

Vienna December 1958	VPO	LP: HMV ALP 1765/ASD 330 LP: EMI XLP 30077/SXLP 30077/SMVP 8061

A Midsummer Night's Dream: Overture, Nocturne, Scherzo and Wedding March

London January 1961	RPO	LP: HMV ALP 1892/ASD 449 LP: Angel 60056 LP: World Records T 736/ST 736

WOLFGANG AMADEUS MOZART (1756-1791)

Symphony No 34

London November 1955	Philharmonia	LP: HMV ALP 1471/MFP 2082 LP: Electrola E 80454 LP: Capitol G 7150/SG 7150 CD: Testament awaiting publication

Symphony No 39

London May-June 1956	RPO	CD: Testament awaiting publication
London June 1956	Philharmonia	HMV unpublished <u>Recording incomplete</u>

Symphony No 41 "Jupiter"

London April-May 1956	RPO	CD: Testament awaiting publication

Piano Concerto No 27

Düsseldorf	Munich PO	LP: BASF 29 21770
November 1972	Gulda	LP: Metronom/Amadeo 149.034

The 4 Horn Concerti

London	RPO	LP: World Records T 628/ST 628
November 1966	Civil	LP: Victor LM 2973/LSC 2973
		LP: EMI EMX 2007
		CD: EMI CDEMX 2007/CDM 769 2812

Rondo for horn and orchestra K371

London	RPO	LP: World Records T 628/ST 628
November 1966	Civil	LP: Victor LM 2973/LSC 2973
		LP: EMI EMX 2007
		CD: EMI CDEMX 2007/CDM 769 2812

Serenade No 13 "Eine kleine Nachtmusik"

London	Philharmonia	LP: HMV BLP 1088
November 1955		LP: Electrola E 70045
1963	Bamberg SO	LP: Eurodisc 70654KK/27642XAK
		LP: Oriole RM 202/RM 52202
		LP: World Records T 437/ST 437
		LP: Realm RM 52176

Cosl fan tutte, Overture

London	Philharmonia	LP: HMV BLP 1088
December 1955		LP: Electrola E 70045

Idomeneo, Overture

London	Philharmonia	45: HMV 7ER 5074
December 1955		

Le Nozze di Figaro, Overture

London	Philharmonia	LP: HMV BLP 1088
December 1955		LP: Electrola E 70045

Die Zauberflöte, Overture

London	Philharmonia	45: HMV 7ER 5074
December 1955		LP: HMV BLP 1088
		LP: Electrola E 70045

Requiem

Berlin	BPO	LP: HMV ALP 1444
June–	St Hedwig's Choir	LP: Electrola E 80006/1C 047 00128M
October 1955	Grümmer, Höffgen,	LP: Capitol G 7113
	Krebs, Frick	CD: EMI CDH 565 2022

OTTO NICOLAI (1810–1849)

Die lustigen Weiber von Windsor, Overture

Vienna	VPO	LP: HMV ALP 1765/ASD 330/SMVP 8061
December 1958		LP: EMI XLP 30077/SXLP 30077

JACQUES OFFENBACH (1819–1880)

Orphée aux enfers, Overture

Vienna	VPO	LP: HMV ALP 1974/ASD 525
December 1960		LP: EMI XLP 30077/SXLP 30077
		CD: Toshiba Shinseido SGR 8008

HANS PFITZNER (1869-1949)

Palestrina: Excerpts (Schlecht lohnt' ich Euch; Der letzte Freund)

Salzburg August 1955	VPO Lorenz, Schöffler	CD: Myto CDM 92259

AMILCARE PONCHIELLI (1834-1886)

La Gioconda, Dance of the hours

Vienna December 1961	VPO	LP: HMV ALP 1974/ASD 525

OTTORINO RESPIGHI (1879-1936)

Pini di Roma

London May 1964	RPO	LP: Reader's Digest RD 4151 LP: Quintessence PMC 7005 CD: Chesky CD 18

EMIL VON REZNICEK (1860-1945)

Donna Diana, Overture

Vienna January 1958	VPO	LP: HMV ALP 1657/ASD 279 LP: Electrola E 80455/STE 80455/ E 41142/STE 41142 LP: Capitol G 7167/SG 7167 LP: Angel 6069 LP: EMI XLP 30060/SXLP 30060 LP: EMI 1C 151 01463-01463

NIKOLAI RIMSKY-KORSAKOV (1844-1908)

Scheherazade

London	RPO	LP: World Records T 657/ST 657
November 1966		LP: EMI CFP 174

FRANZ SCHMIDT (1874-1939)

Notre Dame, Intermezzo

Vienna	VPO	LP: HMV ALP 1974/ASD 525
December 1961		

OTHMAR SCHOECK (1886-1957)

Vom Fischer und syner Fru, cantata

Munich	Munich PO	LP: BASF EA 22 823
1975	Lövaas, Laubenthal, Nimsgern	

FRANZ SCHUBERT (1797-1828)

Symphony No 8 "Unfinished"

June 1963	Bamberg SO	LP: Eurodisc 70470KK/27642XAK
		LP: Oriole RM 201/RM 52201
		LP: World Records T 437/ST 437

Symphony No 9 "Great"

Munich	Munich PO	LP: CBS 72710/78210
May 1968		

Rosamunde: Overture, Entr'acte No 3 and Ballet music No 2

Vienna	VPO	LP: HMV ALP 1910/ASD 478
December 1961		LP: Electrola E 80732/STE 80732
		LP: Angel 35746

ROBERT SCHUMANN (1810-1856)

Symphony No 1 "Spring"

Berlin	BPO	LP: HMV ALP 1581
June 1955		LP: Electrola E 70005
		LP: Capitol G 7117

Piano Concerto

Munich	Munich PO	LP: CBS 72713
May 1968	Freire	

Manfred, Overture

Berlin	BPO	LP: HMV ALP 1581
November-		LP: Electrola E 60094
December 1956		LP: Capitol G 7117

DIMITRI SHOSTAKOVICH (1906-1975)

Symphony No 9

Zürich	Tonhalle-Orchester	Unpublished radio broadcast
February 1974		

BEDRICH SMETANA (1824-1884)

The Bartered Bride

Bamberg	Bamberg SO	LP: HMV ALP 1971-1973/ASD 522-524
May and	RIAS Choir	LP: Electrola E 91226-8/STE 91226-8
June 1962	Lorengar, Wagner,	LP: Angel 3642
and Berlin	Wunderlich, Frick,	LP: EMI HQS 1132-1134
October 1962	Cordes, Sardi	LP: EMI 1C 153 28922-28923
	Sung in German	CD: EMI CDS 749 2792/CHS 764 0022
		Excerpts
		LP: Electrola E 80746/STE 80746
		LP: EMI 1C 063 29002/EX 29 09883
		CD: EMI CZS 767 1872

The Bartered Bride, Overture

Vienna	VPO	LP: HMV ALP 1765/ASD 330/SMVP 8061
December 1958		LP: EMI XLP 30077/SXLP 30077
		CD: Toshiba Shinseido SGR 8008
London	RPO	LP: HMV ALP 1880/ASD 449/SXLP 30125
February-		LP: Angel 60098
April 1961		CD: EMI CDCFP 4587/CDZ 568 7362

The Bartered Bride: Polka, Furiant and Dance of the Comedians

London	RPO	LP: HMV ALP 1880/ASD 449/SXLP 30125
February-		LP: Angel 60098
April 1961		CD: EMI CDCFP 4587/CDZ 568 7362

The Bartered Bride: Excerpt (Alone at last!/Ah bitterness!)

Berlin	BPO	LP: Electrola E 80027/WCLP 548
July 1957	Lindermeier	
	Sung in German	

From Bohemia's Woods and Fields (Ma Vlast)

June 1963	Bamberg SO	LP: Eurodisc 70655KK
		LP: Oriole RM 202/RM 52202
		LP: World Records T 424/ST 424

JOHANN STRAUSS I (1804-1849)

Radetzky March

Vienna	VPO	LP: HMV ALP 1861/ASD 431
February 1958		LP: EMI XLP 30060/SXLP 30060
		LP: EMI 1C 151 01463-01464
		CD: EMI CDZ 767 5882

JOHANN STRAUSS II (1825-1899)

Die Fledermaus, Overture

Vienna	VPO	LP: HMV ALP 1637/ASD 279
January 1958		LP: Electrola E 80455/STE 80455
		LP: Capitol G 7167/SG 7167
		LP: EMI XLP 30083/SXLP 30083
		LP: EMI 1C 151 01463-01464
		LP: Angel 6109
		CD: EMI CDZ 762 8552
		CD: Laserlight 16207
Dresden	Dresden	LP: Eurodisc 86847IU
September 1973	Staatskapelle	LP: RCA LRL1-5044
		LP: Eterna 845 105
		CD: Berlin Classics BC 90072

G'schichten aus dem Wienerwald, waltz

Vienna	VPO	LP: HMV ALP 1861/ASD 431
December 1960		LP: EMI XLP 30060/SXLP 30060
		LP: Angel 35851/6109
		LP: EMI 1C 151 01463-01464
		CD: EMI CDZ 762 8552
		CD: Laserlight 16207
Dresden	Dresden	LP: Eurodisc 86847IU
September 1973	Staatskapelle	LP: RCA LRL1-5044
		LP: Eterna 845 105
		CD: Berlin Classics BC 90752/90072

Im Krapfenwaldl, polka

Vienna	VPO	LP: HMV ALP 1861/ASD 431
December 1960		LP: EMI XLP 30083/SXLP 30083
		LP: Angel 35851/6109
		LP: EMI 1C 151 01463-01464
		CD: EMI CDZ 762 8552
		CD: Laserlight 16207

Kaiserwalzer

Vienna	VPO	LP: HMV ALP 1861/ASD 431
December 1960		LP: EMI XLP 30083/SXLP 30083
		LP: Angel 35851/6109
		LP: EMI 1C 151 01463-01464
		CD: EMI CDZ 762 8552
		CD: Laserlight 16207

Leichtes Blut, polka

Vienna	VPO	LP: HMV ALP 1861/ASD 431
December 1960		LP: EMI XLP 30060/SXLP 30060
		LP: Angel 35851/6109
		LP: EMI 1C 151 01463-01464
		CD: EMI CDZ 762 8552
		CD: Laserlight 16207
Dresden	Dresden	LP: Eurodisc 86847IU
September 1973	Staatskapelle	LP: RCA LRL1-5044
		LP: Eterna 845 105
		CD: Berlin Classics BC 90072

1001 Nacht, Intermezzo

Vienna	VPO	LP: HMV ALP 1861/ASD 431
December 1960		LP: EMI XLP 30083/SXLP 30083
		LP: Angel 35851/6109
		LP: EMI 1C 151 01463-01464
		CD: EMI CDZ 762 8552
		CD: Laserlight 16207

JOSEF STRAUSS (1827-1870)

Dynamiden, waltz

Vienna	VPO	LP: HMV ALP 1861/ASD 431
December 1960		LP: EMI XLP 30083/SXLP 30083
		LP: Angel 35851/6109
		LP: EMI 1C 151 01463-01464
		CD: EMI CDZ 762 8552
		CD: Laserlight 16207

Sphärenklänge, waltz

Vienna January 1958	VPO	LP: HMV ALP 1637/ASD 279 LP: Electrola E 80455/STE 80455 LP: Capitol G 7167/SG 7167 LP: EMI XLP 30060/SXLP 30060 LP: Angel 6109 LP: EMI 1C 151 01463-01464 CD: EMI CDZ 762 8552 CD: Laserlight 16207
Dresden September 1973	Dresden Staatskapelle	LP: Eurodisc 86847IU LP: RCA LRL1-5044 LP: Eterna 845 105 CD: Berlin Classics BC 90072

RICHARD STRAUSS (1864-1949)

Arabella

New York February 1955	Metropolitan Opera Orchestra & Chorus Steber, Güden, Peters, Thebom, Sullivan, London Sung in English	Unpublished Met broadcast US premiere performances

Arabella: Excerpt (Und du wirst mein Gebieter sein)

London 1953	Bavarian State Orchestra Della Casa, Uhde	LP: Melodram MEL 094 Guest performance by Bayerische Staatsoper

Ariadne auf Naxos

Dresden June-July 1968	Dresden Staatskapelle Janowitz, Geszty, Zylis-Gara, King, Schreier, Prey, Adam	LP: EMI SAN 215-217/SLS 936 LP: EMI 1C 165 00110-00112 LP: Eterna 820 009-820 011 CD: EMI CMS 764 1592 Excerpts LP: EMI 1C 063 00824/100 8241

Elektra

London May 1958	Covent Garden Orchestra Lammers, Milinkovic, Müller-Bütow, E.Evans, O.Kraus	Unpublished radio broadcast

Capriccio, Mondscheinmusik

Dresden June 1970	Dresden Staatskapelle	LP: Eterna 826 439

Feuersnot

Munich 1958	Bavarian State Orchestra & Chorus Cunitz, Ostertag, Cordes, Proebstl, Engen	LP: Melodram MEL 103

Die Frau ohne Schatten

Munich August 1954	Bavarian State Orchestra & Chorus Rysanek, Schech, Köth, Benningsen, Hopf, Metternich, Böhme	LP: Melodram MEL 108

Intermezzo, Act 2 Prelude (Entr'acte)

Dresden June 1970- September 1971	Dresden Staatskapelle	EMI unpublished

Josephslegende, Ballet in one act

Dresden March 1974	Dresden Staatskapelle	LP: EMI SLS 894/1C 195 52100-52102 LP: Eterna 826 627 CD: EMI CMS 764 3462

Der Rosenkavalier

Dresden 1950	Dresden Staatskapelle and Chorus Bäumer, Lemnitz, U.Richter, Löbel, Böhme	LP: Urania 201/9201/Nixa 52014 LP: Acanta JA 23039 Excerpts LP: Urania 602/7062/8010 LP: Urania 9602/58010 LP: Saga XID 5177 LP: Historia H 704-705

Der Rosenkavalier, Waltz sequences

Dresden June 1973	Dresden Staatskapelle	LP: EMI SLS 880/ASD 3074 LP: EMI 1C 195 50344-50346 LP: Angel 37046 LP: Eterna 826 624 CD: EMI CMS 764 3462/CZS 568 1102

Salome

Orange July 1974	Orchestre National Rysanek, Hesse, Vickers, Laubental, Stewart	LP: HRE Records HRE 396

Salome, closing scene

Vienna September 1951	VPO Welitsch	Unpublished video recording Promotional film

Salome, Dance of the seven veils

Dresden June 1970	Dresden Staatskapelle	LP: EMI SLS 894/1C 195 52100-52102 LP: EMI ESD 7026/ED 29 00531/1C 063 02344' LP: Eterna 826 437 LP: Angel 60297 CD: EMI CMS 764 3462/CDC 747 8652 CD: EMI CZS 568 1102

Schlagobers, Waltz from the ballet

Dresden September 1971	Dresden Staatskapelle	LP: EMI SLS 861/1C 191 50271-50274 LP: Eterna 826 439 CD: EMI CMS 764 3462

Eine Alpensinfonie

London April 1966	RPO	LP: RCA RB 6696/SB 6696 LP: RCA LM 2923/LSC 2923 LP: RCA (Germany) 26.41092
Dresden September 1971	Dresden Staatskapelle	LP: EMI SLS 861/ASD 3173/1C 063 02341 LP: EMI 1C 191 50271-50274 LP: Eterna 826 440 CD: EMI CMS 764 3502

Also sprach Zarathustra

Dresden	Dresden	LP: EMI SLS 861/1C 191 50271-50274
September 1971	Staatskapelle	LP: EMI ESD 7026/ED 29 08011
		LP: Eterna 826 438
		LP: Angel 60283
		LP: EMI 1C 063 02342
		CD: EMI CMS 764 3462/CDC 747 8622
		CD: EMI CZS 568 1102

Aus Italien

Dresden	Dresden	LP: EMI SLS 894/1C 195 52100-52102
March 1974	Staatskapelle	LP: Eterna 826 628
		LP: Angel 60301
		LP: EMI 1C 063 02523
		CD: EMI CMS 764 3502

Le bourgeois gentilhomme, Suite of incidental music

Dresden	Dresden	LP: EMI SLS 861/1C 195 50271-50274
June 1970	Staatskapelle	LP: Eterna 826 439
		CD: EMI CMS 764 3462

Burleske for piano and orchestra

Dresden	Dresden	LP: EMI SLS 5067/1C 191 02743-02746
September 1975	Staatskapelle	LP: Eterna 826 553
	Frager	LP: Angel 32767
		CD: EMI CMS 764 3422

Don Juan

London	RPO	LP: Reader's Digest RD 4151
May 1964		LP: Quintessence PMC 7005
		CD: Menuet 681102
		CD: Chesky CD 88

Dresden	Dresden	LP: EMI SLS 861/1C 191 50271-50274
June 1970	Staatskapelle	LP: EMI ED 29 00531/1C 063 02342
		LP: Eterna 826 438
		LP: Angel 60288
		CD: EMI CMS 764 3422/CDC 747 8652
		CD: EMI CZS 568 1102

Don Quixote

Berlin June 1958	BPO Tortelier	LP: HMV ALP 1759/ASD 326/CFP 40372 LP: Electrola E 80438/STE 80438 LP: Capitol G 7190/SG 7190 LP: World Records T 609/ST 609 LP: Angel 60122 CD: EMI CDZ 568 7362
Munich December 1966	Bavarian RO Tortelier	CD: Orfeo C267 921B
Dresden June 1973	Dresden Staatskapelle Tortelier	LP: EMI SLS 880/ASD 3074/ED 29 08011 LP: EMI 1C 195 50344-50346 LP: Angel 37046 LP: Eterna 826 624 CD: EMI CMS 764 3502/CDC 747 8652

Duett-Concertino for clarinet and bassoon

Dresden September 1975	Dresden Staatskapelle Weise, Liebscher	LP: EMI SLS 5067/1C 191 02743-02746 LP: Eterna 826 855 CD: EMI CMS 764 3422/CDM 769 6612

Ein Heldenleben

Dresden March 1972	Dresden Staatskapelle	LP: EMI SLS 880/1C 195 50344-50346 LP: Eterna 826 625 LP: Angel 60315 CD: EMI CMS 764 3422/CDM 769 1712 CD: EMI CZS 568 1102
London September 1974	RPO	Unpublished radio broadcast

Horn Concerto No 1

London April 1967	RPO	LP: Reader's Digest RD 4601
Dresden September 1975	Dresden Staatskapelle Damm	LP: EMI SLS 5067/1C 191 02743-02746 LP: EMI 1C 063 02743 LP: Eterna 826 854 LP: Angel 37004 CD: EMI CMS 764 3422/CDM 769 6612

Horn Concerto No 2

Dresden September 1975	Dresden Staatskapelle Damm	LP: EMI SLS 5067/1C 191 02743-02746 LP: EMI 1C 063 02743 LP: Eterna 826 854 LP: Angel 37004 CD: EMI CMS 764 3422/CDM 769 6612

Macbeth

Dresden January 1973	Dresden Staatskapelle	LP: EMI SLS 861/1C 191 50271-50274 LP: Eterna 826 626 LP: Angel 60288 CD: EMI CMS 764 3502/CDM 769 1712

Metamorphosen

Munich May 1968	Munich PO	LP: CBS 72711
Dresden January 1973	Dresden Staatskapelle	LP: EMI SLS 861/1C 191 50271-50274 LP: Eterna 826 626 CD: EMI CMS 764 3502

Oboe Concerto

Dresden September 1975	Dresden Staatskapelle Clement	LP: EMI SLS 5067/ESD 7026 LP: EMI 1C 191 02743-02746 LP: Eterna 826 855 CD: EMI CMS 764 3422/CDM 769 6612

Panathenäenzug for piano and orchestra

Dresden January 1976	Dresden Staatskapelle Rösel	LP: EMI SLS 5067/1C 191 02743-02746 LP: Eterna 826 856 CD: EMI CMS 764 3422

Parergon zur Sinfonia Domestica, for piano and orchestra

Dresden January 1976	Dresden Staatskapelle Rösel	LP: EMI SLS 5067/1C 191 02743-02746 LP: Eterna 826 856 CD: EMI CMS 764 8422

Sinfonia Domestica

Dresden	Dresden	LP: EMI SLS 894/1C 195 52100-52102
March 1972	Staatskapelle	CD: EMI CMS 764 3462

Tanzsuite aus Couperin

Dresden	Dresden	LP: EMI SLS 880/1C 195 50344-50346
December 1972-	Staatskapelle	LP: Eterna 826 627
June 1973		CD: EMI CMS 764 3502

Till Eulenspiegels lustige Streiche

Berlin	BPO	LP: HMV ALP 1759/ASD 326/CFP 40372
June 1958		LP: Electrola E 80438/STE 80438
		LP: Capitol G 7190/SG 7190
		LP: World Records T 609/ST 609
		LP: Angel 60122
		CD: EMI CDZ 568 7362
Dresden	Dresden	LP: EMI SLS 894/ESD 7026/ED 29 00531
June 1970	Staatskapelle	LP: EMI 1C 195 52100-52102/1C 063 02344
		LP: Eterna 826 437
		LP: Angel 60279
		CD: EMI CMS 764 3422/CDC 747 8622
		CD: EMI CZS 568 1102

Tod und Verklärung

Dresden	Dresden	LP: EMI SLS 880/ED 29 00531
June 1970	Staatskapelle	LP: EMI 1C 195 50344-50346/1C 063 02344
		LP: Eterna 826 437
		LP: Angel 60279
		CD: EMI CMS 764 3462/CDC 747 8622
		CD: EMI/CZS 568 1102
		Excerpt
		CD: EMI CHS 565 0582

Violin Concerto

Dresden	Dresden	LP: EMI SLS 5067/1C 191 02743-02746
September 1975	Staatskapelle	LP: Eterna 826 553
	Hoelscher	LP: Angel 3267
		CD: EMI CMS 764 3462

IGOR STRAVINSKY (1882-1971)

L'oiseau de feu, Suite

Dresden January 1976	Dresden Staatskapelle	LP: Eterna 827 012 CD: Berlin Classics BC 10972

FRANZ VON SUPPE (1919-1895)

Morning Noon and Night in Vienna, Overture

Vienna January 1958	VPO	LP: HMV ALP 1637/ASD 279 LP: Electrola E 80455/STE 80455 LP: Capitol G 7167/SG 7167 LP: EMI XLP 30060/SXLP 30060 LP: EMI 1C 151 01463-01464 LP: Angel 6109
Dresden September 1973	Dresden Staatskapelle	LP: Eurodisc 86847IU LP: RCA LRL1-5044 LP: Eterna 845 105 CD: Berlin Classics BC 90752/BC 90072

PIOTR TCHAIKOVSKY (1840-1893)

Symphony No 5

Berlin May 1959	BPO	LP: HMV ALP 1800/ASD 379 LP: Electrola E 80509/STE 80509 LP: Capitol G 7219/SG 7219 LP: World Records T 673/ST 673 LP: EMI SXLP 30126/CFP 41 44781
London August 1964	LSO	Unpublished radio broadcast
Date not confirmed	Bavarian RO	CD: Originals SH 809

Symphony No 6 "Pathétique"

London May 1957	Philharmonia	LP: HMV ALP 1566 LP: Capitol G 7128

A version of Tchaikovsky Symphony 4, in which Kempe conducts the Bamberg SO, was published in USA in cassette form, Encore EC 5013

Piano Concerto No 1

Munich	Munich PO	LP: CBS 72712/78210/61697/31041
May 1968	Freire	

Violin Concerto

Rome	RAI Roma Orchestra	CD: Hunt CDLSMH 34015
1959	D.Oistrakh	
Turin	RAI Torino	CD: Live Classic Best (Japan) LCB 125
April 1963	Orchestra	CD: Frequenz 041.011
	D.Oistrakh	

Theme and Variations (Suite No 3)

Vienna	VPO	LP: HMV ALP 1930/ASD 494
December 1961		LP: Angel 35975
		LP: World Records T 763/ST 763

Eugene Onegin: Excerpt (Tatiana's Letter scene)

Berlin	BPO	LP: Electrola E 80440/E 80027/WCLP 548
July 1957	Lindermeier	
	Sung in German	

Eugene Onegin, Waltz and Polonaise

Berlin	BPO	LP: Electrola E 80440/E 80027/WCLP 548
July 1957	Deutsche Oper	LP: EMI 1C 151 30641-30642 (Polonaise)
	Chorus	
	Sung in German	

RICHARD WAGNER (1813-1883)

Der fliegende Holländer, Overture

Berlin November- December 1956	BPO	LP: HMV ALP 1513/XLP 30040 LP: Electrola E 80016 LP: Angel 35574 CD: Testament SBT 1035

Götterdämmerung

London October 1957	Covent Garden Orchestra & Chorus Nilsson, Lindermeier, Svanholm, Uhde, Frick	Unpublished radio broadcast
Bayreuth August 1960	Bayreuth Festival Orchestra & Chorus Nilsson, Bjoner, G.Hoffman, Hopf, Stewart, Frick, O.Kraus	LP: Melodram MEL 609

Götterdämmerung, Dawn and Siegfried's Rhine Journey

Berlin November- December 1956	BPO	LP: HMV ALP 1513/XLP 30040 LP: Electrola E 80016 LP: Angel 35574 CD: Testament SBT 1035

Lohengrin

Munich 1952	Bavarian State Orchestra & Chorus Schech, Klose, Vincent, A.Boehm, Böhme, Wolff	LP: Urania 225 LP: Nixa ULP 9225 LP: Acanta 40 223264 CD: Pilz 44 21182/44 21332 Excerpts LP: Urania 7077/7123 LP: Vox OPL 110/PL 15150 LP: Saga XID 5117
Vienna November- December 1962 and April 1963	VPO Vienna Opera Chorus Grümmer, C.Ludwig, Thomas, Frick, Fischer-Dieskau, Wiener	LP: EMI AN 121-125/SAN 121-125/SLS 5071 LP: EMI 1C 161 00017-00020/EX 29 09553 LP: Angel 3641 CD: EMI CDS 749 0178 Excerpts LP: EMI SME 80853/1C 063 00747 CD: EMI CDZ 762 8562

Lohengrin, Act 1 Prelude

Vienna February 1958	VPO	LP: HMV ALP 1638/XLP 30048 LP: Electrola E 80456 LP: Capitol G 7180/SG 7180 CD: EMI CDZ 762 8562

Die Meistersinger von Nürnberg

Dresden 1951	Dresden Staatskapelle and Chorus Lemnitz, Walther-Sack, Unger, Aldenhoff, Frantz, Böhme, Pflanzl, Faulhaber	LP: Urania URLP 206 LP: Vox OPBX 142 LP: BASF 22 292673 Excerpts LP: Urania 7067/7077 LP: Vox OPL 350/PL 15100 LP: Saga XID 5117/XID 5290/STXID 5290 LP: Acanta DE 29269
New York January 1956	Metropolitan Opera Orchestra & Chorus Della Casa, Glatz, Da Costa, Franke, Schöffler, Tozzi, Pechner	Unpublished Met broadcast Excerpts CD: Melodram CDM 26526
Berlin April 1956	BPO Deutsche Oper and Staatsoper Choirs St Hedwig's Choir Grümmer, Höffgen, Unger, Schock, Frantz, Frick, Wilhelm, Kusche	LP: HMV ALP 1506-1510/HQM 1094-1098 LP: Electrola E 90008-90012 LP: Angel 3572 LP: Eterna 820 108-820 112 LP: EMI RLS 740 CD: EMI CMS 764 1542 Excerpts LP: Electrola E 60094/WDLP 557/SME 80923 LP: EMI ALP 2253/1C 063 00746 CD: Testament SBT 1035 CD: EMI CDEMX 2228

Die Meistersinger von Nürnberg, Overture

Düsseldorf November 1972	Munich PO	LP: BASF 29 217701

Parsifal, Prelude and Karfreitagszauber

Vienna January 1958	VPO	LP: HMV ALP 1638/XLP 30048 LP: Electrola E 80456 LP: Capitol G 7180/SG 7180 CD: EMI CDZ 762 8562

Das Rheingold

Bayreuth July 1960	Bayreuth Festival Orchestra Bjoner, Töpper, Höffgen, H.Kraus, Stolze, Paskuda, Hines, Stewart, Van Mill, Roth-Ehrang	LP: Melodram MEL 606

Das Rheingold, scenes (Prelude, Scene 1 and Scene 4)

Berlin March 1959	Staatskapelle and Chorus Blatter, Siewert, Schock, Melchert, Frantz, Metternich, Kusche	LP: HMV ALP 1984/ASD 535/CFP 109 LP: Electrola E 80470/STE 80470 LP: Eterna 825 091 CD: Berlin Classics BC 20035 CD: EMI CMS 565 2122

Siegfried

Bayreuth July 1960	Bayreuth Festival Orchestra Nilsson, Siebert, Höffgen, Hopf, H.Kraus, Uhde, O.Kraus, Roth-Ehrang	LP: Melodram MEL 608 Excerpt LP: Melodram MEL 094

Tannhäuser

New York January 1955	Metropolitan Opera Orchestra & Chorus Varnay, Krall, Thebom, Vinay, London, Hines	LP: Raritas OPR 409 LP: Melodram MEL 038

Tannhäuser, Overture and Venusberg music

Berlin November- December 1956	BPO Deutsche Oper Chorus	LP: HMV ALP 1513/XLP 30040 LP: Electrola E 80016 LP: Angel 35574 CD: Testament SBT 1035

Tristan und Isolde, Prelude and Liebestod

Vienna January 1958	VPO	LP: HMV ALP 1638/XLP 30048 LP: Electrola E 80456 LP: Capitol G 7180/SG 7180 CD: EMI CDZ 762 8562

Tristan und Isolde: Excerpts (Die alte Weise/Das Schiff? Siehst du's noch nicht?)

Berlin 1954	Staatskapelle Seider, Hotter	LP: Melodram MEL 668

Die Walküre

Bayreuth July 1960	Bayreuth Festival Orchestra Varnay, Töpper, Nordmo-Lövberg, Windgassen, Hines, Frick	LP: Melodram MEL 607

CARL MARIA VON WEBER (1786-1826)

Der Freischütz

Dresden 1951	Dresden Staatskapelle and Chorus Trötschel, Beilke, Aldenhoff, Böhme, Faulhaber	LP: Urania URLP 403/242-243/5242-5243 LP: Vox OPBX 149 LP: BASF 22 292681 <u>Excerpts</u> LP: Vox OPL 260

Euryanthe, Overture

June 1963	Bamberg SO	LP: Eurodisc 70654KK/87372XBK/47400NK LP: Oriole RM 202/RM 52202

Oberon, Overture

Vienna January 1958	VPO	LP: HMV ALP 1765/ASD 330/SMVP 8061 LP: EMI XLP 30077/SXLP 30077 CD: EMI CDZ 568 7362

JAROMIR WEINBERGER (1896-1967)

Schwanda der Dudelsackpfeifer, Polka and Fugue

London	RPO	LP: HMV ALP 1880/ASD 449/SXLP 30125
January 1961		LP: Angel 60098
		CD: EMI CDCFP 4587

ERMANNO WOLF-FERRARI (1876-1948)

Violin Concerto in D

Munich	Munich PO	LP: Thomas Clear TLC 2583
November 1972	Bustabo	CD: Classic Record ACR 37

INTERVIEWS WITH RUDOLF KEMPE

New York 1956
Munich 1964-1974
London 1975

LP: Orfeo S079 832I
<u>Munich interviews are in German, the others in English</u>

Joseph Keilberth
1908-1968

Discography compiled
by John Hunt

LUDWIG VAN BEETHOVEN (1770-1827)

Symphony No 1

Bamberg	Bamberg SO	LP: Telefunken LT 43007/GMA 20/SMA 20
July 1958		LP: Telefunken AH 641.339

Symphony No 2

Bamberg	Bamberg SO	LP: Telefunken LT 43049/GMA 20/SMA 20
July 1958		LP: Telefunken AH 641.339

Symphony No 3 "Eroica"

Hamburg	Philharmonisches	LP: Telefunken LSK 7035/GMA 1/SMA 1
October 1956	Staatsorchester	CD: Teldec 2292 424662

Symphony No 4

Hamburg	Philharmonisches	LP: Telefunken LT 6633
September 1958	Staatsorchester	

Symphony No 5

Hamburg	Philharmonisches	LP: Telefunken LSK 7021/LGX 66005
January 1953	Staatsorchester	
Hamburg	Philharmonisches	LP: Telefunken TW 30172/GMA 2/SMA 2
February 1958	Staatsorchester	CD: Teldec ZS 844.069/9031 748192

Symphony No 6 "Pastoral"

Bamberg	Bamberg SO	LP: Telefunken LT 43050/AH 641.330
July 1960		CD: Teldec 9031 748192

Symphony No 7

Berlin May 1960	BPO	LP: Telefunken LT 43041/GMA 88/SMA 88 LP: Telefunken AH 642.150/SLT 43041 CD: Teldec 9031 738622
Munich 1967	Bavarian RO	CD: Orfeo C268 921B

Symphony No 8

Hamburg February 1958	Philharmonisches Staatsorchester	LP: Telefunken TW 30150/GMA 20/SMA 20
Munich 1967	Bavarian RO	CD: Orfeo C268 921B

Symphony No 9 "Choral"

Tokyo 1965	NHK Orchestra and Chorus Ito, Kurimoto, Mori, Kunikaza	CD: Seven Seas (Japan) 270 E15

Piano Concerto No 5 "Emperor"

Stockholm 1959	Stockholm PO Backhaus	LP: Paragon DSV 52012

Violin Concerto

Paris May 1967	Orchestre National Ferras	CD: Disques Montaigne TCE 8720 CD: Frequenz 041.019

Coriolan Overture

Bamberg March 1952	Bamberg SO	78: Telefunken E 3916/VSK 9025 LP: Telefunken TM 68002
Bamberg July 1960	Bamberg SO	LP: Telefunken SNT 1085/DM 648.163 CD: Teldec 2292 242662
Munich 1967	Bavarian RO	CD: Orfeo C268 921B

Egmont Overture

Berlin 1941	BPO	78: Telefunken E 1181/VSK 9025 LP: Capitol (USA) P 8164
Berlin April– May 1960	BPO	LP: Telefunken LT 43041/TM 68002/ SLT 43041/GMA 88/SMA 88/ Telefunken AH 642.150/DM 648.163 CD: Teldec 9031 738622

Fidelio Overture

Bamberg July 1960	Bamberg SO	LP: Telefunken SNT 1085/DM 648.163 CD: Teldec 2292 242662

Fidelio: Excerpt (Ha, welch ein Augenblick!)

Dresden 1946	Dresden Staatskapelle J. Herrmann	LP: Eterna 820 960

Fidelio: Excerpt (O namenlose Freude!)

Dresden 1946	Dresden Staatskapelle Goltz, Aldenhoff	LP: BASF 72 221792

Leonore No 3 Overture

Berlin 1941	BPO	LP: Capitol (USA) P 8164
Bamberg March 1952	Bamberg SO	78: Telefunken VSK 9013 LP: Telefunken TW 30005
Berlin April 1960	BPO	LP: Telefunken SLT 43051/DM 648.163 CD: Teldec 9031 738622

Die Ruinen von Athen, Turkish March

Hamburg April 1960	Philharmonisches Staatsorchester	LP: Telefunken SLT 43051/DM 648.163 CD: Teldec 2292 242662

JOHANNES BRAHMS (1833-1897)

Symphony No 1

Berlin March 1951	BPO	LP: Telefunken LSK 7008/LGX 66003 LP: Capitol (USA) P 8153 CD: Teldec 9031 738612
Tokyo 1968	NHK Orchestra	CD: Seven Seas (Japan) 270 E16

Symphony No 2

Berlin 1965-1966	BPO	LP: Telefunken AH 642.323/GMA 87/SMA 87 CD: Teldec 9031 738614/9031 738673 CD: Teldec 2292 424652
Munich 1960	Bavarian RO	CD: Refrain (Japan) DR 92 0036

Symphony No 3

Hamburg November 1952	Philharmonisches Staatsorchester	LP: Telefunken LSK 7020/LGX 66035
Bamberg July 1957	Bamberg SO	LP: Telefunken NT 846/GMA 89/SMA 89 LP: Telefunken AF 641.349/AH 641.349 CD: Teldec 9031 738672/2292 424652

Symphony No 4

Hamburg	Philharmonisches	LP: Telefunken LT 43042/AH 641.841
April 1960	Staatsorchester	

Academic Festival Overture

Bamberg	Bamberg SO	LP: Telefunken LB 6015/LGM 65007
March 1952		

Tragic Overture

Bamberg	Bamberg SO	LP: Telefunken TW 30215
July 1957		

Hungarian Dances Nos 1, 3 and 10

Bamberg	Bamberg SO	LP: Telefunken NT 846/GMA 89/SMA 89
July 1957		LP: Telefunken AF 641.349

MAX BRUCH (1838-1920)

Violin Concerto No 1

Berlin	BPO	78: Telefunken SK 3172-3174
June 1941	Kulenkampff	CD: Teldec 9031 764432
		CD: Alta Nova CDAN 1

ANTON BRUCKNER (1824-1896)

Symphony No 4 "Romantic"

Tokyo 1968	NHK Orchestra	CD: Seven Seas (Japan) 270 E17

Symphony No 6

Berlin 1965-1966	BPO	LP: Telefunken AN 641.168 LP: Telefunken GMA 83/SMA 83 CD: Teldec ZK 843.194

Symphony No 7

Tokyo 1968	NHK Orchestra	CD: Seven Seas (Japan) 270 E18

Symphony No 9

Hamburg October 1956	Philharmonisches Staatsorchester	LP: Telefunken LSK 7034/LGX 66072 LP: Telefunken GMA 104/SMA 104 LP: Telefunken AH 641.149 CD: Teldec 2292 424632

ANTONIN DVORAK (1841-1904)

Symphony No 9 "From the New World"

Bamberg 1957-1958	Bamberg SO	LP: Telefunken GMA 67/AH 641.338 CD: Teldec 9031 738662

Cello Concerto

Hamburg October 1958	Philharmonisches Staatsorchester Hoelscher	LP: Telefunken LT 6629/GMA 9/SMA 9

Carnival Overture

Bamberg 1957-1958	Bamberg SO	LP: Telefunken GMA 67/AH 641.338 CD: Teldec 9031 738662

Slavonic Dances op 46: Nos 1,3,4,6 and 8

Bamberg October 1956	Bamberg SO	LP: Telefunken TW 30116/GMA 11/SMA 11

Slavonic Dances op 72: Nos 1,2,4,7 and 8

Bamberg October 1956	Bamberg SO	LP: Telefunken TW 30124/GMA 11/SMA 11

Rusalka

Dresden 1950-1952	Dresden Staatskapelle and Chorus Trötschel, Otto, Schindler, Frick, Lange, Rott Sung in German	LP: Urania URLP 219/US 5219 Excerpt LP: BASF 72 221792

WERNER EGK (1901-1983)

Die Zaubergeige, Overture

Prague	Deutsches	78: Telefunken SK 3700
December 1941-	Philharmonisches	78: Capitol (USA) 8-86012
December 1942	Orchester	

WILHELM FURTWAENGLER (1886-1954)

Symphony No 3, unfinished version

| Bamberg | Bamberg SO | Unpublished radio broadcast |
| 1956 | | <u>Closing bars also on unpublished video recording</u> |

CHRISTOPH WILLIBALD GLUCK (1714-1787)

Alceste Overture

Prague	Deutsches	78: Urania 7028
1943	Philharmonisches	LP: Melodiya M10 46259 002
	Orchester	<u>Melodiya incorrectly names orchestra as Bamberg SO</u>

Iphigenie in Aulis, Overture

Prague	Deutsches	LP: Melodiya M10 46259 002
1943	Philharmonisches	<u>Melodiya incorrectly names orchestra as Bamberg SO</u>
	Orchester	

Ballet Suite, arranged by Mottl

Prague	Deutsches	78: Urania 7018
1943	Philharmonisches	
	Orchester	

JAKOV GOTOVAC (born 1895)

Sinfonischer Kolo

Date not confirmed	Deutsches Philharmonisches Orchester	78: Telefunken E 3136

CHARLES GOUNOD (1818-1893)

Faust

Stuttgart December 1937	Reichssender Orchestra & Chorus Teschemacher, Waldenau, Rosvaenge, Nissen, Hann Sung in German	CD: Preiser 90040 Also issued on LP by Preiser

JOSEF HAYDN (1732-1809)

Symphony No 85 "La reine"

Bamberg July 1957	Bamberg SO	LP: Telefunken LT 6615/GMA 29/SMA 29

Symphony No 101 "The Clock"

Prague June 1941	Deutsches Philharmonisches Orchester	78: Telefunken E 3233-3235
Bamberg July 1957 and January 1959	Bamberg SO	LP: Telefunken LT 6615/SLT 43015 LP: Telefunken GMA 29/SMA 29

Die Schöpfung

Cologne December 1957	WDR Orchestra and Chorus Kupper, Traxel, Greindl, Berry	LP: Melodram MEL 231

PAUL HINDEMITH (1895-1963)

Cardillac

Cologne June 1968	WDR Orchestra and Chorus Söderström, Kirschstein, Grobe, Fischer-Dieskau	LP: DG 2707 042/2721 246 CD: DG 431 7412 <u>Excerpt</u> LP: DG 2705 001

Symphonic Metamorphoses on a theme by Weber

Hamburg September 1955	Philharmonisches Staatsorchester	LP: Telefunken LE 6554/LGX 66055 LP: Telefunken BLE 43062/GMA 24 LP: Telefunken DP 648.019

Nobilissima Visione

Hamburg September 1955	Philharmonisches Staatsorchester	LP: Telefunken LE 6554/LGX 66055 LP: Telefunken BLE 43062/GMA 24 LP: Telefunken DP 648.019

LEOS JANACEK (1854-1928)

The Excursions of Mr Broucek

Cologne September 1959	WDR Orchestra and Chorus Lipp, Fahberg, Benningsen, Fehenberger, Wunderlich, Kuen, Alexander <u>Sung in German</u>	Unpublished radio broadcast
Munich November 1959	Bavarian State Orchestra & Chorus Lipp, Fahberg, Benningsen, Fehenberger, Wunderlich, Kuen, Böhme <u>Sung in German</u>	CD: Orfeo C354 942I <u>German stage premiere</u>

GUSTAV MAHLER (1860-1911)

Symphony No 8 "Symphony of a Thousand"

Vienna June 1960	VSO Wiener Singverein Muszely, Scheyrer, Lipp, Rössel-Majdan, Boese, Wunderlich, Prey, Edelmann	Unpublished radio broadcast

Das Lied von der Erde

Bamberg April 1964	Bamberg SO Wunderlich, Fischer-Dieskau	Unpublished private recording
Vienna June 1964	VSO Wunderlich, Fischer-Dieskau	Unpublished radio broadcast

FELIX MENDELSSOHN-BARTHOLDY (1810-1847)

The Hebrides, Overture

Berlin 1965-1966	BPO	LP: Telefunken BA 642.889

Meeresstille glückliche Fahrt, Overture

Berlin 1965-1966	BPO	LP: Telefunken BA 642.889

WOLFGANG AMADEUS MOZART (1756-1791)

Symphony No 28

Bamberg   Bamberg SO   LP: Telefunken GMA 76
1956-1958

Symphony No 29

Paris   Bamberg SO   LP: Oiseau Lyre OL 50005
1953

Symphony No 30

Bamberg   Bamberg SO   LP: Telefunken TW 30154/TM 68007/LGX 68007
February 1953

Symphony No 33

Prague   Deutsches   Telefunken unpublished
December 1941   Philharmonisches
                   Orchester

Symphony No 35 "Haffner"

Bamberg   Bamberg SO   LP: Telefunken GMA 90/SMA 90
1956-1958

Symphony No 36 "Linz"

Bamberg   Bamberg SO   LP: Telefunken GMA 90/SMA 90
1956-1958

Symphony No 38 "Prague"

Prague June 1941	Deutsches Philharmonisches Orchester	78: Telefunken E 3208-3210
Bamberg November 1955	Bamberg SO	LP: Telefunken LT 43012/LGX 66054 LP: Telefunken GMA 17/SMA 17/DT 648.109 CD: Teldec 9031 748212

Symphony No 39

Prague 1941	Deutsches Philharmonisches Orchester	78: Telefunken E 3105-3107
Bamberg November 1955	Bamberg SO	LP: Telefunken LT 43012/LGX 66054 LP: Telefunken GMA 17/SMA 17/DT 648.109 CD: Teldec 9031 748212

Symphony No 40

Bamberg July 1959	Bamberg SO	LP: Telefunken LT 6636/GMA 39/SMA 39 LP: Telefunken DT 648.109/AH 641.842 CD: Teldec 9031 738652
Munich December 1966	Bavarian RO	CD: Refrain (Japan) DR 92 0036

Symphony No 41 "Jupiter"

Bamberg July 1959	Bamberg SO	LP: Telefunken LT 6636/GMA 39/SMA 39 LP: Telefunken DT 648.109/AH 641.842 CD: Teldec 9031 738652

Divertimento No 1

Bamberg July 1959	Bamberg SO	LP: Telefunken GMA 33 CD: Teldec 9031 738692

Divertimento No 2

Bamberg 1956-1958	Bamberg SO	LP: Telefunken GMA 76 CD: Teldec 9031 738692

Serenade No 6 "Serenata notturna"

Bamberg 1956-1958	Bamberg SO	LP: Telefunken GMA 76 CD: Teldec 9031 738692

Serenade No 13 "Eine kleine Nachtmusik"

Bamberg February 1953	Bamberg SO	78: Telefunken VE 9028 LP: Telefunken TW 30001/TW 30154
Bamberg July 1959	Bamberg SO	LP: Telefunken TW 30230/TM 68010 LP: Telefunken LGX 66025/GMA 33 CD: Teldec 9031 738692

Notturno for 4 orchestras

Bamberg July 1959	Bamberg SO	LP: Telefunken GMA 33 CD: Teldec 9031 748212

2 Minuets K403

Bamberg July 1959	Bamberg SO	LP: Telefunken GMA 33

6 German Dances K509

Paris 1953	Bamberg SO	LP: Oiseau Lyre OL 50005
Bamberg July 1959	Bamberg SO	LP: Telefunken GMA 33/GMA 90/SMA 90

6 German Dances K571

Paris 1953	Bamberg SO	LP: Oiseau Lyre OL 50005

La Clemenza di Tito

Cologne December 1955	WDR Orchestra and Chorus Zadek, Malaniuk, Gedda, Offermanns, Gröschel, Wallenstein <u>Sung in German</u>	LP: Cetra LO 78

Don Giovanni

Stuttgart March 1936	Reichssender Orchestra & Chorus Reining, Jungkurth, Callam, Patzak, Hammes, Hann, Ducrue <u>Sung in German</u>	CD: Preiser 90263

Don Giovanni: Excerpts (Notte e giorno fatigar; Ah fuggi il traditor!; La ci darem la mano; Fin ch' han del vino; Don Giovanni, a cenar teco!.... to end of opera)

Munich August 1962	Munich PO Bavarian State Chorus Jurinac, Hillebrecht, Rothenberger, Gedda, London, Frick, Kusche	LP: Orfeo S120 842I

Der Schauspieldirektor, Overture

Bamberg July 1959	Bamberg SO	LP: Telefunken GMA 33

Die Zauberflöte

Stuttgart December 1937	Reichssender Orchestra & Chorus Eipperle, Piltti, Preisig, W.Ludwig, Manowarda, Hann, Schmitt-Walter	CD: Preiser 90254 <u>Conclusion of opera missing and spliced in from another recording</u>
Cologne December 1954	WDR Orchestra and Chorus Stich-Randall, Lipp, Schick, Kunz, Greindl, Hotter	Unpublished radio broadcast
Salzburg August 1960	VPO Vienna Opera Chorus Fölser, Köth, Sciutti, Wunderlich, Berry, Frick, Wächter	Unpublished radio broadcast

<u>Haffner Serenade and Zauberflöte Overture may also have been recorded for Telefunken with Bamberg SO</u>

HANS PFITZNER (1869-1949)

Von deutscher Seele

Munich December 1965	Bavarian Radio Orchestra & Chorus Giebel, Töpper, Wunderlich, Wiener	LP: DG 2707 027 CD: DG 437 0332

Das Käthchen von Heilbronn, Overture and Epilogue

Prague July 1944	Deutsches Philharmonisches Orchester	78: Telefunken E 3819-3820/E 3582-3583
Bamberg September 1951	Bamberg SO	Catalogue numbers not confirmed

Palestrina, 3 Preludes

Prague December 1942	Deutsches Philharmonisches Orchester	78: Telefunken E 3337 (Prelude 1) 78: Telefunken E 3817-3818 (Prels.2 & 3) 78: Capitol 89.80097-89.80099/ECL 8025 LP: Capitol P 8037

BAYERISCHE STAATSOPER
NATIONALTHEATER MÜNCHEN

Mittwoch, 24. Februar 1965

Der Herr Bundespräsident ist anwesend

Neuinszenierung

TOSCA

Musikdrama in drei Akten von V. Sardou, L. Illica und G. Giacosa

Deutsch von Max Kalbeck

Musik von

GIACOMO PUCCINI

Musikalische Leitung: Joseph Keilberth
Inszenierung: Hans Hartleb
Bühnenbild und Kostüme: Ekkehard Grübler

BAYERISCHE STAATSOPER
NATIONALTHEATER MÜNCHEN

Zum 100. Geburtstag von Richard Strauss

Donnerstag, 11. Juni 1964

ELEKTRA

Tragödie in einem Aufzug von Hugo von Hofmannsthal

Musik von

RICHARD STRAUSS

Musikalische Leitung: Joseph Keilberth
Inszenierung: Hans Hartleb
Bühnenbild: Helmut Jürgens † · Kostüme: Liselotte Erler

MAX REGER (1873-1916)

Ballet Suite for orchestra

Bamberg 1953	Bamberg SO	LP: Telefunken TK 11520/GMA 81

Böcklin-Suite

Prague December 1942	Deutsches Philharmonisches Orchester	78: Telefunken SK 3464-3466 78: Telefunken GX 61010-61012 78: Capitol 89.80029-89.80031/ECL 8007 LP: Capitol L 8011

Variations and Fugue on a theme of Hiller

Hamburg March 1955	Philharmonisches Staatsorchester	LP: Telefunken UE 6540/BLE 43064 LP: Telefunken TK 11520/LGX 66049/GMA 72

Variations and Fugue on a theme of Mozart

Prague December 1941	Deutsches Philharmonisches Orchester	Catalogue number not confirmed
Bamberg 1954	Bamberg SO	LP: Telefunken TK 11520/GMA 81

GIOACHINO ROSSINI (1792-1868)

Il Barbiere di Siviglia

Munich December 1959	Bavarian State Orchestra & Chorus Köth, Wunderlich, Prey, Proebstl, Hotter <u>Sung in German</u>	Unpublished video recording

FRANZ SCHUBERT (1797-1828)

Symphony No 6

Bamberg February 1954	Bamberg SO	LP: Telefunken TW 30161/LGM 65026

Symphony No 8 "Unfinished"

Bamberg February 1954	Bamberg SO	LP: Telefunken TW 30151/LGX 66042/GMA 73
Bamberg July 1960	Bamberg SO	LP: Telefunken TW 30232/AN 641.147 CD: Teldec 9031 738632

ROBERT SCHUMANN (1810-1856)

Symphony No 1 "Spring"

Prague 1942	Deutsches Philharmonisches Orchester	78: Telefunken SK 3832-3835 LP: Capitol (USA) P 8129
Bamberg January 1953	Bamberg SO	LP: Telefunken LS 6041/LGM 65010

Symphony No 4

Prague March 1941	Deutsches Philharmonisches Orchester	78: Telefunken E 3255-3257 LP: Capitol (USA) P 8129 LP: Mercury MG 15001

Cello Concerto

Berlin 1942	Staatskapelle Hoelscher	78: HMV DB 4550-4552 Issued on LP by Capitol (USA)

Piano Concerto

1952	Bamberg SO Schmid	LP: Mercury MG 15020 LP: Royale 1358 Royale edition issued with pseudonyms

BEDRICH SMETANA (1824-1884)

The Bartered Bride

Munich 1958	Bavarian Radio Orchestra & Chorus Siebert, D.Hermann, Ilosvay, Francl, Wehofschitz, H.Braun, Böhme, Schmitt-Walter <u>Sung in German</u>	CD: Panthéon PHE 665 253

From Bohemia's Woods and Fields (Ma Vlast)

Bamberg March 1952	Bamberg SO	LP: Telefunken LB 6014/LGM 65006 LP: Telefunken GMA 68/AN 641.147 CD: Teldec 9031 738632

The Moldau (Ma Vlast)

Bamberg March 1952- February 1954	Bamberg SO	LP: Telefunken LB 6014/LGM 65006/TW 30002 LP: Telefunken GMA 68/GMA 73/AN 641.147 CD: Teldec 9031 738632 <u>Telefunken catalogue no. UV 101 also quoted</u>

JOHANN STRAUSS II (1825-1899)

Accelerationen, waltz

Bamberg July 1960	Bamberg SO	LP: Telefunken GMA 60/SMA 60/AH 641.306 CD: King (Japan) K33Y 10053 CD: Teldec ZK 843.273

Aegyptischer Marsch

Bamberg July 1960	Bamberg SO	LP: Telefunken GMA 60/SMA 60/AH 641.306 CD: King (Japan) K33Y 10053 CD: Teldec ZK 843.273

An der schönen blauen Donau, waltz

Bamberg July 1957	Bamberg SO	LP: Telefunken TW 30156/GMA 94/SMA 94

Annen Polka

Bamberg July 1960	Bamberg SO	LP: Telefunken GMA 60/SMA 60/AH 641.306 CD: King (Japan) K33Y 10053 CD: Teldec ZK 843.273

Kaiserwalzer

Bamberg July 1957	Bamberg SO	LP: Telefunken TW 30156/GMA 94/SMA 94

Leichtes Blut, polka

Bamberg July 1960	Bamberg SO	LP: Telefunken GMA 60/SMA 60/AH 641.306 CD: King (Japan) K33Y 10053 CD: Teldec ZK 843.273

Morgenblätter, waltz

Bamberg   Bamberg SO   LP: Telefunken BLE 43054/GMA 94/SMA 94
July 1959

Perpetuum mobile

Bamberg   Bamberg SO   LP: Telefunken GMA 60/GMA 94/SMA 60/SMA 94
July 1960   LP: Telefunken AH 641.306
                                         CD: King (Japan) K33Y 10053
                                         CD: Teldec ZK 843.273

Persischer Marsch

Bamberg   Bamberg SO   LP: Telefunken BLE 43054/GMA 60/SMA 60
July 1959   LP: Telefunken AH 641.306
                                         CD: King (Japan) K33Y 10053
                                         CD: Teldec ZK 843.273

Rosen aus dem Süden, waltz

Bamberg   Bamberg SO   LP: Telefunken BLE 43054/GMA 60/SMA 60
July 1959   LP: Telefunken AH 641.306
                                         CD: King (Japan) K33Y 10053
                                         CD: Teldec ZK 843.273

Tritsch-Tratsch, polka

Bamberg   Bamberg SO   LP: Telefunken BLE 43054/AH 641.306
July 1959   LP: Telefunken GMA 60/GMA 94/SMA 60/SMA 94
                                         CD: King (Japan) K33Y 10053
                                         CD: Teldec ZK 843.273

Wein Weib und Gesang, waltz

Bamberg   Bamberg SO   LP: Telefunken TW 30156/GMA 94/SMA 94
July 1957

Wiener Blut, waltz

Bamberg   Bamberg SO   LP: Telefunken GMA 60/SMA 60/AH 641.306
July 1960   CD: King (Japan) K33Y 10053
                                         CD: Teldec ZK 843.273

RICHARD STRAUSS (1864-1949)

Don Juan

Berlin 1963	BPO	LP: Telefunken GMA 68/SMA 68/BA 642.889

Till Eulenspiegels lustige Streiche

Berlin 1963	BPO	LP: Telefunken GMA 68/SMA 68/BA 642.889

Die Aegyptische Helena

Munich August 1956	Bavarian State Orchestra & Chorus Rysanek, Kupper, Aldenhoff, Holm, Uhde	LP: Ed Smith 268 LP: Melodram MEL 109 CD: Melodram MEL 27066

Arabella

Munich July 1963	Bavarian State Orchestra & Chorus Della Casa, Rothenberger, Paskuda, Kohn, Fischer-Dieskau	LP: DG LPM 18 883-18 885/ SLPM 138 883-138 885 LP: DG 2709 013/2721 163 CD: DG 437 7002 Excerpts LP: DG 136 419/2705 001

Arabella: Excerpts (Mandryka! Der reiche Kerl!; Sie woll'n mich heiraten?)

Salzburg July 1958	VPO Della Casa, Fischer-Dieskau, Edelmann	CD: Orfeo C335 931A

Daphne

Munich September 1964	Bavarian Radio Orchestra & Chorus Woytowicz, Töpper, Wunderlich, King, Frick	Unpublished video recording

Die Frau ohne Schatten

Munich November 1964	Bavarian State Orchestra & Chorus Borkh, Bjoner, Mödl, Thomas, Fischer-Dieskau	LP: DG LPM 18 911-18 914/ SLPM 138 911-138 914 LP: DG 2721 161 Excerpts LP: DG 136 422

Intermezzo

Munich 1963	Bavarian State Orchestra & Chorus Steffek, Kmennt, Gruber, Pernerstorfer, Prey, Welter	LP: Melodram MEL 113

Intermezzo, 4 symphonic interludes

Munich 1962	Bavarian State Orchestra	LP: Telefunken GMA 106/SMA 106/AH 641.164 CD: Teldec ZK 843.446

Der Rosenkavalier

Munich May 1965	Bavarian State Orchestra & Chorus Watson, Töpper, Köth, Wunderlich, Böhme, Wiener	Unpublished radio broadcast Gala performance for Queen Elizabeth II

Der Rosenkavalier, waltz sequences

Munich 1962	Bavarian State Orchestra	LP: Telefunken GMA 106/SMA 106/AH 641.164 CD: Teldec ZK 843.446

Salome

Dresden 1948	Dresden Staatskapelle Goltz, Karen, Aldenhoff, J.Herrmann	LP: Musical Treasures (USA) LP: Oceanic (USA) 302 LP: Olympic 9101 CD: Berlin Classics BC 20622 <u>Excerpts</u> LP: BASF 72 221792
Munich July 1951	Bavarian State Orchestra Borkh, Barth, Lorenz, Hotter	LP: Melodram MEL 106 CD: Orfeo C342 932I

Salome, Dance of the 7 veils

Munich 1962	Bavarian State Orchestra	LP: Telefunken GMA 106/SMA 106/AH 641.164 CD: Teldec ZK 843.446

Die schweigsame Frau, potpourri

Munich 1962	Bavarian State Orchestra	LP: Telefunken GMA 106/SMA 106/AH 641.164 CD: Teldec ZK 843.446

PIOTR TCHAIKOVSKY (1840-1893)

Eugene Onegin

Munich October 1962	Bavarian State Orchestra & Chorus Bremert, Töpper, Fassbaender, Wunderlich, Prey, Yahia Sung in German	Unpublished video recording

GIUSEPPE VERDI (1813-1901)

Aida

Stuttgart April 1938	Reichssender Orchestra & Chorus Teschemacher, Karen, Rosvaenge, Hann, Weber Sung in German	CD: Preiser 90274 Excerpts LP: BASF 72 221792 LP: Bellaphon/Acanta DE 23057

Requiem

Stuttgart November 1938	Reichssender Orchestra Karlsruhe Chorus Teschemacher, Willer, Rosvaenge, Hann	LP: Discophilia K 18-19 LP: Preiser LV 151-152 CD: Preiser 90068

RICHARD WAGNER (1813-1883)

Der fliegende Holländer

Bayreuth July 1955	Bayreuth Festival Orchestra & Chorus Varnay, Schärtel, Traxel, Windgassen, Uhde, Weber	LP: Decca LXT 5150-5152/D97 D3 Also issued on Decca Eclipse LP <u>Excerpts</u> LP: Decca (Germany) BLK 16513
Bayreuth July 1956	Bayreuth Festival Orchestra & Chorus Varnay, Schärtel, Traxel, Cox, London, Van Mill	LP: Melodram MEL 560 CD: Myto MCD 93175 <u>Excerpt</u> LP: Melodram MEL 097

Der fliegende Holländer: Excerpts (Wie aus der Ferne....to end of Act 2; Verloren, ach verloren!....to end of opera)

Bayreuth August 1956	Bayreuth Festival Orchestra Varnay, Traxel, Schöffler, Weber	LP: Melodram MEL 560

Götterdämmerung

Bayreuth August 1952	Bayreuth Festival Orchestra & Chorus Varnay, Mödl, Siewert, Lorenz, Uhde, Greindl, Neidlinger	LP: Melodram MEL 529 CD: Paragon PCD 84025-84028
Bayreuth August 1953	Bayreuth Festival Orchestra & Chorus Mödl, Malaniuk, Hinsch-Grondahl, Windgassen, Uhde, Greindl, Neidlinger	LP: Allegro-Elite 3138-3142 LP: Melodram MEL 539
Bayreuth August 1955	Bayreuth Festival Orchestra & Chorus Varnay, Ilosvay, Brouwenstijn, Windgassen, Uhde, Greindl, Neidlinger	Decca unpublished
Bayreuth August 1955	Bayreuth Festival Orchestra & Chorus Mödl, Ilosvay, Brouwenstijn, Windgassen, Uhde, Greindl, Neidlinger	Decca unpublished

Lohengrin

Bayreuth August 1953	Bayreuth Festival Orchestra & Chorus Steber, Varnay, Windgassen, Uhde, Braun	LP: Decca LXT 2880-2884/D12 D5 CD: Teldec 4509 936742 <u>Excerpts</u> LP: Decca (Germany) BLK 16514/LW 50512

Lohengrin, Preludes Acts 1 and 3

Hamburg January 1957	Philharmonisches Staatsorchester	LP: Telefunken GMA 28/SMA 28

<u>Act 1 Prelude may also have been recorded with Bamberg SO; the choral excerpt
Treulich geführt may have been recorded by Electrola with BPO and Deutsche
Oper Chorus</u>

Die Meistersinger von Nürnberg

Munich November 1963	Bavarian State Orchestra & Chorus Watson, Benningsen, Thomas, Lenz, Wiener, Hotter, Kusche	LP: Eurodisc XI 70851R CD: RCA/BMG GD 69008 <u>Opening performance in the rebuilt</u> <u>Nationaltheater</u>

Die Meistersinger von Nürnberg, Overture

Bamberg March 1952	Bamberg SO	LP: Telefunken LB 6015/LGM 65007
Hamburg January 1957	Philharmonisches Staatsorchester	LP: Telefunken GMA 28/SMA 28

Die Meistersinger von Nürnberg, Act 3 Prelude

Hamburg January 1957	Philharmonisches Staatsorchester	LP: Telefunken GMA 28/SMA 28

Das Rheingold

Bayreuth July 1952	Bayreuth Festival Orchestra Borkh, Malaniuk, Windgassen, Witte, Kuen, Uhde, Weber, Greindl, Neidlinger	LP: Melodram MEL 526 CD: Paragon PCD 84015-84016
Bayreuth August 1953	Bayreuth Festival Orchestra Falcon, Malaniuk, Ilosvay, Witte, Stolze, Kuen, Weber, Uhde, Greindl, Neidlinger	LP: Allegro-Elite 3125-3127 LP: Melodram MEL 536
Bayreuth July 1955	Bayreuth Festival Orchestra Wilfert, Ilosvay, Milinkovic, Traxel, Lustig, Kuen, Weber, Hotter, Greindl, Neidlinger	Decca unpublished
Bayreuth August 1955	Bayreuth Festival Orchestra Wilfert, Ilosvay, Milinkovic, Traxel, Lustig, Kuen, Weber, Hotter, Greindl, Neidlinger	Decca unpublished

Siegfried

Bayreuth July 1952	Bayreuth Festival Orchestra Varnay, Streich, Bugarinovic, Aldenhoff, Kuen, Hotter, Neidlinger, Böhme	LP: Melodram MEL 528 CD: Paragon PCD 84021-84024
Bayreuth August 1953	Bayreuth Festival Orchestra Mödl, Streich, Ilosvay, Windgassen, Kuen, Hotter, Greindl, Neidlinger	LP: Allegro-Elite 3133-3137 LP: Melodram MEL 538
Bayreuth August 1955	Bayreuth Festival Orchestra Varnay, Hollweg, Ilosvay, Windgassen, Kuen, Hotter, Greindl, Neidlinger	Decca unpublished
Bayreuth August 1955	Bayreuth Festival Orchestra Mödl, Hollweg, Ilosvay, Windgassen, Kuen, Hotter, Greindl, Neidlinger	Decca unpublished

Tannhäuser

Bayreuth July 1954	Bayreuth Festival Orchestra & Chorus Brouwenstijn, Wilfert, Vinay, Blankenheim, Fischer-Dieskau, Greindl	LP: Melodram MEL 544 CD: Melodram MEL 36105 <u>Excerpts</u> LP: Gioielli della lirica GML 027

Die Walküre

Bayreuth July 1952	Bayreuth Festival Orchestra Varnay, Borkh, Malaniuk, Treptow, Hotter, Greindl	LP: Melodram MEL 527 CD: Paragon PCD 84017-84020 <u>Act 1</u> LP: Melodram MEL 077
Bayreuth July 1953	Bayreuth Festival Orchestra Mödl, Resnik, Malaniuk, Vinay, Hotter, Greindl	LP: Allegro-Elite 3128-3132 LP: Melodram MEL 537
Bayreuth July 1954	Bayreuth Festival Orchestra Varnay, Mödl, Milinkovic, Lorenz, Hotter, Greindl	LP: Melodram MEL 547 CD: Melodram MEL 36102
Bayreuth July 1955	Bayreuth Festival Orchestra Varnay, Mödl, Milinkovic, Vinay, Hotter, Greindl	LP: Melodram MEL 557
Bayreuth August 1955	Bayreuth Festival Orchestra Mödl, Varnay, Milinkovic, Vinay, Hotter, Greindl	Decca unpublished

Wesendonk-Lieder

Cologne 1955	WDR Orchestra Mödl	LP: Melodram MEL 075

CARL MARIA VON WEBER (1786-1826)

Der Freischütz

Berlin April and September 1958	BPO Deutsche Staatsoper Chorus Grümmer, Otto, Schock, Prey, Kohn, Frick	LP: HMV ALP 1752-1754/ASD 319-321 LP: HMV HQM 1031-1032/HQS 1031-1032 LP: EMI EX 29 06943 CD: EMI CMS 769 3422 Excerpts LP: Electrola E 70418/1C 047 28553 LP: EMI EX 29 12103 CD: EMI CDM 769 1372

Der Freischütz, Overture

Bamberg February 1953	Bamberg SO	78: Telefunken E 9027 LP: Telefunken TM 68015

Euryanthe, Overture

Bamberg February 1953	Bamberg SO	78: Telefunken E 9027 LP: Telefunken TM 68015

HUGO WOLF (1860-1903)

Italian Serenade

Prague March 1941	Deutsches Philharmonisches Orchester	78: Telefunken E 3158 78: Capitol (USA) 8-86003 LP: Capitol (USA) H 8131

Wolfgang Sawallisch
born 1923

Discography compiled
by John Hunt

JOHANN SEBASTIAN BACH (1685-1750)

Brandenburg Concerto No 3

Berlin 1953	Berlin RO	LP: Realm RM 52176 Also issued on LP by Remington

Brandenburg Concerto No 5

Lugano June 1964	Swiss-Italian Radio Orchestra Gay des Combés, Zuppiger, Sgrizzi	CD: Eremitage ERM 154

Transcriptions by Leopold Stokowski: Schafe können sicher weiden, Wachet auf, Ein' feste Burg and Toccata and Fugue in D minor

Collingswood NJ March 1995	Philadelphia Orchestra	CD: EMI CDC 555 5922

BELA BARTOK (1881-1945)

Bluebeard's Castle

Munich March- April 1979	Bavarian State Orchestra Varady, Fischer-Dieskau	LP: DG 2531 172 CD: DG 423 2362

LUDWIG VAN BEETHOVEN (1770-1827)

Symphony No 1

Amsterdam June 1993	Concertgebouw Orchestra	CD: EMI CDC 754 5012

Symphony No 2

Amsterdam June 1993	Concertgebouw Orchestra	CD: EMI CDC 754 5022

Symphony No 3 "Eroica"

Amsterdam June 1993	Concertgebouw Orchestra	CD: EMI CDC 754 5032

Symphony No 4

Lugano June 1964	Swiss-Italian Radio Orchestra	CD: Eremitage ERM 154
Amsterdam November 1991	Concertgebouw Orchestra	CD: EMI CDC 754 5032

Symphony No 5

Tokyo	NHK SO	CD: RCA/BMG VD 60534
Amsterdam March 1991	Concertgebouw Orchestra	CD: EMI CDC 754 5042

Symphony No 6 "Pastoral"

Amsterdam September 1960	Concertgebouw Orchestra	LP: Philips A02026L/835 067AY LP: Philips GL 5808/SGL 5808/SFM 23012
Amsterdam March 1991	Concertgebouw Orchestra	CD: EMI CDC 754 5042

Symphony No 7

Amsterdam January 1962	Concertgebouw Orchestra	LP: Philips A02237L/835 124AY LP: Philips GL 5809/SGL 5809
Amsterdam November 1991	Concertgebouw Orchestra	CD: EMI CDC 754 5032

Symphony No 8

Tokyo	NHK SO	CD: RCA/BMG VD 60534
Amsterdam December 1992	Concertgebouw Orchestra	CD: EMI CDC 754 5022

Symphony No 9 "Choral"

Amsterdam December 1992	Concertgebouw Orchestra Düsseldorf Choir M.Price, Lipovsek, Seiffert, Rootering	CD: EMI CDC 754 5052 <u>Excerpt</u> CD: EMI CDZ 568 0632

Piano Concerto No 5 "Emperor"

London May-June 1982	Philharmonia Egorov	LP: EMI ASD 143 4331 CD: EMI CES 568 5202

Violin Concerto

London 1983	LSO Ughi	CD: RCA/BMG GD 86536/74321 242002

Fidelio, Overture

Amsterdam September 1960	Concertgebouw Orchestra	45: Philips 400 227AE/740 024AV LP: Philips A02026L/835 067AY LP: Philips GL 5808/SGL 5808

King Stephen, Overture

Amsterdam September 1960	Concertgebouw Orchestra	45: Philips 400 227AE/740 024AV LP: Philips A01137L/835 124AY LP: Philips GL 5809/SGL 5809

Leonore No 2, Overture

Munich 1981	Bavarian State Orchestra	CD: Orfeo C161 871R

First movement of Moonlight Sonata, transcribed by Stokowski

Collingswood NJ March 1995	Philadelphia Orchestra	CD: EMI CDC 555 5922

LUIGI BOCCHERINI (1743-1805)

Minuet, transcribed by Stokowski

Collingswood NJ March 1995	Philadelphia Orchestra	CD: EMI CDC 555 5922

ALEXANDER BORODIN (1833-1887)

In the Steppes of Central Asia

Munich November 1987	Bavarian State Orchestra	CD: EMI CDD 763 8932

JOHANNES BRAHMS (1833-1897)

Symphony No 1

Vienna December 1962	VSO	LP: Philips GL 5799/SGL 5799/6752 001 LP: Metronome/Juwel 140.127 CD: Philips 438 7572
London April 1991	LPO	CD: EMI CDC 754 3592/CMS 764 5192

Symphony No 2

Vienna January 1959	VSO	LP: Philips ABL 3286/SABL 120/A02025L LP: Philips GL 5800/SGL 5800/6752 001 LP: Metronome/Juwel 140.128 CD: Philips 438 7572
London June 1989	LPO	CD: EMI CDC 754 0592/CMS 764 5192

Symphony No 3

Vienna January 1961	VSO	LP: Philips GL 5801/SGL 5801/6752 001 LP: Metronome/Juwel 140.165 CD: Philips 438 7572
London December 1991	LPO	CD: EMI CDC 754 5232/CMS 764 5192

Symphony No 4

Vienna February 1963	VSO	LP: Philips 6752 001/6580 024 LP: Philips GL 5802/SGL 5802 LP: Metronome/Juwel 140.182 CD: Philips 438 7572
London June 1989	LPO	CD: EMI CDC 754 0602/CMS 764 5192

Piano Concerto No 1

London December 1991	LPO Kovacevich	CD: EMI CDC 754 5782

Piano Concerto No 2

London December 1993	LPO Kovacevich	CD: EMI CDC 555 2182

Violin Concerto

London August 1983	Philharmonia Ughi	CD: RCA/BMG RD 70072/VD 60605/VD 60479 CD: RCA/BMG 74321 292452
Berlin January 1995	BPO Zimmermann	CD: EMI CDC 555 4262

Double Concerto

Philadelphia 1995	Philadelphia Orchestra Zimmermann, Schiff	EMI awaiting publication

Haydn Variations

Vienna November 1959	VSO	LP: Philips A02025L/6752 001 LP: Philips GL 5803/SGL 5803 LP: Metronome/Juwel 140.128 CD: Philips 438 7602
London April 1990	LPO	CD: EMI CDC 754 0592/CMS 764 5192 CD: EMI CDZ 568 0632

Academic Festival Overture

Vienna January 1961	VSO	LP: Philips 6752 001/6580 024 LP: Philips GL 5800/SGL 5800 LP: Metronome/Juwel 140.182 CD: Philips 438 7602
London April 1991	LPO	CD: EMI CDC 754 5232/CMS 764 5191

Tragic Overture

Vienna April 1961	VSO	LP: Philips GL 5801/SGL 5801/6752 001 LP: Metronome/Juwel 140.165 CD: Philips 438 7602
Munich 1981	Bavarian State Orchestra	CD: Orfeo C161 871A
London April 1990	LPO	CD: EMI CDC 754 0602

Ein deutsches Requiem

Vienna February 1962	VSO Wiener Singverein Lipp, Crass	LP: Philips 02226-02227L/835 114-835 115AY LP: Philips 6720 006/6780 018 LP: Philips SFL 14057-14058 CD: Philips 438 7602
Munich October 1983	Bavarian Radio Orchestra & Chorus M.Price, Allen	CD: Orfeo C039 101A Performance dedicated to Karl Richter

Alto Rhapsody

Vienna February 1962	VSO Wiener Singverein Heynis	LP: Philips 02226-02227L/835 114-835 115AY LP: Philips GL 5803/SGL 5803 LP: Philips 6780 018/SFL 14057-14058 CD: Philips 438 7602

Schicksalslied

Vienna February 1962	VSO Wiener Singverein	LP: Philips 02226-02227L/835 114-835 115AY LP: Philips GL 5803/SGL 5803 LP: Philips 6780 018/SFL 14057-14058 CD: Philips 438 7602

ANTON BRUCKNER (1824-1896)

Symphony No 1

Munich October 1984	Bavarian State Orchestra	CD: Orfeo C145 851A

Symphony No 4 "Romantic"

Philadelphia March 1993	Philadelphia Orchestra	CD: EMI CDC 555 1192

Symphony No 5

Munich	Bavarian State Orchestra	CD: Orfeo C241 911A

Symphony No 6

Munich October 1981	Bavarian State Orchestra	CD: Orfeo C024 821A

Symphony No 9

Munich December 1984	Bavarian State Orchestra	CD: Orfeo C160 851A

FREDERIC CHOPIN (1810-1849)

Prelude in E minor, transcribed by Stokowski

Collingswood NJ March 1995	Philadelphia Orchestra	CD: EMI CDC 555 5922

CLAUDE DEBUSSY (1862-1918)

Transcriptions by Stokowski: Clair de lune; La cathédrale engloutie

Collingswood NJ March 1995	Philadelphia Orchestra	CD: EMI CDC 555 5922

ANTONIN DVORAK (1841-1904)

Symphony No 7

Philadelphia April 1989	Philadelphia Orchestra	CD: EMI CDC 749 9482/CMS 764 8122

Symphony No 8

London June 1954	Philharmonia	LP: Columbia 33SX 1034
Philadelphia April 1989	Philadelphia Orchestra	CD: EMI CDC 749 9482/CMS 764 8122

Symphony No 9 "From the New World"

London February 1958	Philharmonia	LP: Columbia 33CX 1677/SAX 2322 LP: EMI CFP 104/1C 037 11641
Philadelphia April 1988	Philadelphia Orchestra	CD: EMI CDC 749 1142/CMS 764 8122

Cello Concerto

Philadelphia February 1991	Philadelphia Orchestra Gutman	CD: EMI CDC 754 3202/CMS 764 8122

Symphonic Variations

Philadelphia February 1991	Philadelphia Orchestra	CD: EMI CDC 754 3202

Scherzo capriccioso

London June 1954	Philharmonia	LP: Columbia 33SX 1034
Philadelphia April 1988	Philadelphia Orchestra	CD: EMI CDC 749 1142/CDZ 568 0632

Carnival, Overture

London	Philharmonia	LP: Columbia 33CX 1677/SAX 2322
February 1958		LP: EMI CFP 104/1C 037 11641

Slavonic Dances

Prague	Czech PO	VHS Video: EMI MVD 491 1373
March 1993		Laserdisc: EMI LDB 491 1371

Requiem

Prague	Czech Philharmonic	CD: Supraphon 10 4241-2232
May 1984	Orchestra & Chorus	
	Benackova,	
	Fassbaender,	
	T.Moser, Rootering	

Stabat mater

Prague	Czech Philharmonic	LP: Supraphon 11 123561-11 123562
1983	Orchestra & Chorus	CD: Supraphon 10 3561-2232
	Benackova, Wenkel,	
	Dvorsky, Rootering	

CESAR FRANCK (1822-1890)

Panis angelicus, transcribed by Stokowski

Collingwood NJ	Philadelphia	CD: EMI CDC 555 5922
March 1995	Orchestra	

WILHELM FURTWAENGLER (1886-1954)

Symphony No 3, unfinished version

Munich	Bavarian State	LP: French Furtwängler Society SWF 8603
January 1980	Orchestra	

MIKHAIL GLINKA (1804-1857)

Russlan and Ludmilla, Overture

Munich	Bavarian State	CD: EMI CDD. 763 8932
November 1987	Orchestra	

GEORGE FRIDERIC HANDEL (1685-1759)

Concerto grosso op 6 no 5

Berlin 1953	Berlin RO	LP: Remington

Music for the Royal Fireworks

Munich 1973	Bavarian State Wind Ensemble	LP: EMI 1C 065 28941

JOSEF HAYDN (1732-1809)

Symphony No 94 "Surprise"

Vienna April 1961	VSO	LP: Philips 6527 034 CD: Philips 422 9732/432 2192

Symphony No 100 "Military"

Vienna April 1961	VSO	LP: Philips 6527 034 CD: Philips 422 9732/432 2192

Symphony No 101 "Clock"

Vienna October 1962	VSO	LP: Philips 6747 057 CD: Philips 422 9732/432 2192

Divertimento No 46 in B flat

Munich 1973	Bavarian State Wind Ensemble	LP: EMI 1C 065 28941

<u>Haydn Symphony No 92 "Oxford" may also have been recorded with Vienna Symphony Orchestra</u>

PAUL HINDEMITH (1895-1963)

Mathis der Maler, Symphony

Philadelphia April-May 1994	Philadelphia Orchestra	CD: EMI CDC 555 2302

Nobilissima Visione

New Jersey October 1994	Philadelphia Orchestra	CD: EMI CDC 555 2302

Requiem For Those We Love

Vienna November 1983	VSO Vienna Opera Chorus Fassbaender, Fischer-Dieskau	LP: Orfeo S112 851A CD: Orfeo C112 851A

Symphonic Metamorphoses on themes by Weber

Philadelphia April-May 1994	Philadelphia Orchestra	CD: EMI CDC 555 2302

DIMITRI KABALEVSKY (1904-1987)

The Comedians, Suite

Munich November 1987	Bavarian State Orchestra	CD: EMI CDD 763 8932

RUGGIERO LEONCAVALLO (1858-1919)

I Pagliacci, excerpts

Munich 1954	Bavarian Radio Orchestra & Chorus Lipp, Hopf, Pease, Braun <u>Sung in German</u>	LP: Melodram MEL 412

ALBERT LORTZING (1801-1851)

Der Wildschütz, Overture

Munich October 1953	Bamberg SO	78: DG 72 453 45: DG EPL 30 043 LP: DG LPEM 19 009

Der Wildschütz: Excerpt (Wie freundlich strahlt/Heiterkeit und Fröhlichkeit)

Munich October 1953	Bamberg SO Günter	LP: DG LPEM 19 009

PIETRO MASCAGNI (1863-1945)

Cavalleria rusticana

Munich 1954	Bavarian Radio Orchestra & Chorus Varnay, Münch, Schlott, Hopf, Pease <u>Sung in German</u>	LP: Melodram MEL 412

Cavalleria rusticana: Excerpts (Il cavallo scalpita; Voi lo sapete; Oh, il signore vi manda)

Munich October 1953	Bamberg SO Bavarian State Chorus Schech, Pease	LP: DG LPE 17 009 <u>Versions sung in German</u> LP: DG LPEM 19 011 <u>LPEM 19 011 contains other excerpts not conducted by Sawallisch</u>

BOHUSLAV MARTINU (1890-1959)

Cello Concerto No 1

Geneva 1978	Suisse Romande Orchestra Fournier	CD: Cascavelle VEL 2009

FELIX MENDELSSOHN-BARTHOLDY (1809-1847)

Symphony No 1

London June 1967	New Philharmonia Orchestra	LP: Philips 802 856-802 857LY LP: Philips AXS 4004/6700 023 LP: Philips 6707 005/6768 030 CD: Philips 432 5982

Symphony No 2 "Lobgesang"

London June 1967	New Philharmonia Orchestra & Chorus Donath, Hansmann, Kmennt	LP: Philips 802 856-802 857LY LP: Philips AXS 4004/6700 023 LP: Philips 6707 005/6768 030 CD: Philips 432 5982
Berlin September 1987	BPO Düsseldorf Choir Laki, Shirai, Seiffert	CD: EMI CDC 749 7642

Symphony No 3 "Scotch"

London June 1967	New Philharmonia Orchestra	LP: Philips AXS 4004/SAL 3739/6707 005 CD: Philips 432 5982

Symphony No 4 "Italian"

Vienna	VSO	LP: Philips ABL 3285/SABL 120/6530 006
London June 1966	New Philharmonia Orchestra	LP: Philips AXS 4004/SAL 3727/6707 005 LP: Philips 6833 063/412 0081 CD: Philips 422 4702/432 5982/434 5362

Symphony No 5 "Reformation"

London June 1966	New Philharmonia Orchestra	LP: Philips AXS 4004/SAL 3727 LP: Philips 6707 005/412 0081 CD: Philips 422 4702/432 5982/434 5362

Violin Concerto

London June 1954	Philharmonia Martzy	LP: Lexington (Japan) CD: Lexington (Japan)

Elijah

Leipzig June 1968	Gewandhaus- Orchester Leipzig Radio Chorus Ameling, Burmeister, Schreier, Adam Sung in German	LP: Philips 802 889-802 891LY/9802 889 CD: Philips 420 1062/438 3682 Excerpts LP: Philips 6527 146

Ruy Blas, Overture

London June 1967	New Philharmonia Orchestra	LP: Philips AXS 4004/SAL 3739/6707 005

WOLFGANG AMADEUS MOZART (1756-1791)

Symphony No 38 "Prague"

Prague   Czech PO   CD: Eurodisc VD 69253
1984

Symphony No 39

Prague   Czech PO   CD: Eurodisc VD 69253
1984

Symphony No 40

Prague   Czech PO   CD: Eurodisc VD 69253
1984

Symphony No 41 "Jupiter"

Prague   Czech PO   CD: Eurodisc VD 69253
1984

Piano Concerto No 17

London   Philharmonia   LP: EMI EL 27 03621
February 1985   Egorov

Piano Concerto No 20

London   Philharmonia   LP: EMI EL 27 03621
February 1985   Egorov   CD: EMI CES 568 5202

Piano Concerto No 21

London   Philharmonia   LP: Columbia 33CX 1630
February-   A.Fischer   LP: Columbia (Germany) C 90996
March 1958   LP: EMI SXLP 30124
                                       CD: EMI CDZ 767 0022/CES 568 5292

Piano Concerto No 22

London	Philharmonia	LP: Columbia 33CX 1630
March 1958	A.Fischer	LP: Columbia (Germany) C 90996
		LP: EMI SXLP 30124
		CD: EMI CDZ 767 0022/CES 568 5292

Violin Concerto No 3

London	Philharmonia	LP: Lexington (Japan)
June 1954	Martzy	CD: Lexington (Japan)
Berlin	BPO	CD: EMI CDC 555 4262
1994	Zimmermann	

Serenade No 10 for wind instruments, excerpts

Munich	Bavarian State	LP: EMI 1C 065 28941
1973	Wind Ensemble	

Die Zauberflöte

Vienna 1963	VSO Wiener Singverein Mechera, Holm, Wilhelm, Crass, Wächter	Unpublished video recording
Salzburg July 1967	VPO Vienna Opera Chorus Donath, Geszty, Schreier, Prey, Crass, Wiener	Unpublished radio broadcast
Salzburg August 1970	VPO Vienna Opera Chorus Donath, Geszty, Schreier, Prey, Moll, Wiener	Unpublished radio broadcast
Munich August 1972	Bavarian State Orchestra & Chorus Rothenberger, Moser, Schreier, Berry, Moll, Adam	LP: EMI 1C 197 30154-30156 LP: Angel 3807 CD: EMI CDS 747 8278 Excerpts CD: EMI CDM 769 6072/CDZ 568 0632
Rome February 1979	Bavarian State Orchestra & Chorus Wise, Otto, Schreier, Brendel, Moll, Hillebrandt	Unpublished radio broadcast Guest performance by Bavarian State Opera
Munich September 1983	Bavarian State Orchestra & Chorus Popp, Gruberova, Araiza, Brendel, Moll, Böhme	VHS Video: Philips 070 4053 Laserdisc: Philips 070 4051
Tokyo October 1991	NHK SO & Chorus Carter, Brown, Lippert, Helm, Moll	Unpublished video recording

Die Zauberflöte, Overture

Munich 1981	Bavarian State Orchestra	CD: Orfeo C161 871A

BAYERISCHE STAATSOPER
NATIONALTHEATER MÜNCHEN

Staatsoperndirektor Wolfgang Sawallisch

MÜNCHNER OPERNFESTSPIELE 1984

Mittwoch, 11. Juli 1984

Neuinszenierung

Der Barbier von Bagdad

Komische Oper in zwei Aufzügen
von Peter Cornelius

Musikalische Leitung: Wolfgang Sawallisch
Inszenierung: Otto Schenk
Bühnenbild und Kostüme: Rolf Langenfass
Chöre: Günther Schmidt-Bohländer

BAYERISCHE STAATSOPER

NATIONALTHEATER MÜNCHEN

Donnerstag, 12. April 1979

PARSIFAL

Ein Bühnenweihfestspiel in drei Aufzügen

von

RICHARD WAGNER

Musikalische Leitung: Wolfgang Sawallisch

Nach der Inszenierung von Dietrich Haugk · Spielleitung: Oscar Arnold-Paur

Bühnenbild: Günther Schneider-Siemssen · Kostüme: Bernd Müller, Jörg Neumann

Chöre: Wolfgang Baumgart

MODEST MUSSORGSKY (1839-1881)

Night on Bare Mountain

Munich November 1987	Bavarian State Orchestra	CD: EMI CDD 763 8932/CDEMX 2255

OTTO NICOLAI (1810-1849)

Die lustigen Weiber von Windsor, Overture

Munich October 1953	Bamberg SO	78: DG 72 453 45: DG EPL 30 043

CARL ORFF (1895-1982)

Carmina burana

Cologne June 1956	WDR Orchestra and Chorus Giebel, Kuen, Cordes	LP: Columbia 33CX 1480 LP: Columbia (Germany) C 90283 CD: EMI CDM 764 2372

Die Kluge

London May 1956	Philharmonia Schwarzkopf, Christ, Cordes, Frick, Prey	LP: Columbia 33CX 1446-7/SAX 2257-8 LP: Columbia (Germany) C 90284-90285/ STC 90284-90285 LP: Angel 3551 LP: EMI 1C 137 43291-43293 LP: Arabesque 8021-8022 CD: EMI CMS 763 7122 <u>Excerpts</u> LP: Columbia 33CX 1810/SAX 2456 LP: EMI 1C 063 00719 CD: EMI CZS 767 1872

Der Mond

London March 1957	Philharmonia Orchestra & Chorus Christ, Kuen, Schmitt-Walter, Peter, Hotter	LP: Columbia 33CX 1534-1535 LP: Columbia (Germany) C 90288-90289 LP: Angel 3567 LP: EMI 1C 137 43291-43293 CD: EMI CMS 763 7122 <u>Excerpts</u> LP: Columbia 33CX 1811/SAX 2457 LP: EMI 1C 063 01136

NICOLO PAGANINI (1782-1840)

Violin Concerto No 1

Philadelphia 1994	Philadelphia Orchestra Chang	CD: EMI CDC 555 0262

HANS PFITZNER (1869-1949)

Das Käthchen von Heilbronn, Overture

Munich November 1984	Bavarian RO	CD: Orfeo C168 881A

Palestrina, 3 Preludes

Munich November 1984	Bavarian RO	CD: Orfeo C168 881A

Die Rose vom Liebesgarten, Blütenwunder und Trauermarsch

Munich November 1984	Bavarian RO	CD: Orfeo C168 881A

7 Gesänge für Bariton und Orchester

Munich March 1979	Bavarian RO Fischer-Dieskau	LP: EMI 1C 065 45616 LP: EMI EX 29 04353 (selection)

SERGEI PROKOFIEV (1891-1953)

The Love of Three Oranges, March and Scherzo

Munich November 1987	Bavarian State Orchestra	CD: EMI CDD 763 8932

SERGEI RACHMANINOV (1873-1943)

Prelude in C sharp minor, transcribed by Stokowski

Collingswood NJ March 1995	Philadelphia Orchestra	CD: EMI CDC 555 5922

NIKOLAI RIMSKY-KORSAKOV (1844-1908)

Capriccio espagnol

Munich November 1987	Bavarian State Orchestra	CD: EMI CDD 763 8932

GIOACHINO ROSSINI (1792-1868)

Mosè

Rome April 1968	RAI Roma Orchestra & Chorus Zylis-Gara, Lane, Verrett, Corradi, Garaventa, Petri, Ghiaurov	LP: Estro Armonico EA 048 CD: Hunt CDMP 491 Excerpts CD: Memories HR 4223-4224

Petite messe solennelle

Baumburg Chiemgau July 1972	Munich Vocal Soloists Lövaas, Fassbaender, Schreier, Fischer-Dieskau	LP: RCA/Ariola MLDS 60006 CD: Eurodisc 610.263 232

CAMILLE SAINT-SAENS (1835-1921)

Havanaise for violin and orchestra

Philadelphia 1994	Philadelphia Orchestra Chang	CD: EMI CDC 555 0262

Introduction and Rondo capriccioso for violin and orchestra

Philadelphia 1994	Philadelphia Orchestra Chang	CD: EMI CDC 555 0262

FRANZ SCHUBERT (1797-1828)

Symphony No 1

Dresden 1966	Dresden Staatskapelle	LP: Philips SBAL 40/6747 491 CD: Philips 446 5362

Symphony No 2

Lugano June 1964	Swiss-Italian Radio Orchestra	CD: Eremitage ERM 154
Dresden 1966	Dresden Staatskapelle	LP: Philips SBAL 40/6747 491 CD: Philips 446 5362

Symphony No 3

Dresden 1966	Dresden Staatskapelle	LP: Philips SBAL 40/6747 491 CD: Philips 446 5362

Symphony No 4 "Tragic"

Dresden 1966	Dresden Staatskapelle	LP: Philips SBAL 40/6747 491 CD: Philips 422 9772/446 5362

Symphony No 5

Dresden 1966	Dresden Staatskapelle	LP: Philips SBAL 40/SAL 3679 LP: Philips 6747 491/6527 050 CD: Philips 446 5392

Symphony No 6

Dresden 1966	Dresden Staatskapelle	LP: Philips SBAL 40/SAL 3679/6747 491 CD: Philips 6747 491

Symphony No 8 "Unfinished"

Vienna	VSO	LP: Philips ABL 3285/SABL 120/SDAL 501
Dresden 1966	Dresden Staatskapelle	LP: Philips SBAL 40/SAL 3672 LP: Philips 6747 491/6527 050 CD: Philips 422 9772/446 5392

Symphony No 9 "Great"

Dresden 1966	Dresden Staatskapelle	LP: Philips SBAL 40/6747 491 CD: Philips 446 5392

Symphony No 9 "Great", excerpts

Date not confirmed	Bavarian RO	CD: RCA/BMG GD 60054 <u>Soundtrack to a TV documentary about</u> <u>Schubert; film directed by Fritz Lehner</u>

Overture in the Italian style D590

Dresden 1966	Dresden Staatskapelle	LP: Philips SBAL 40/SAL 3672/6747 491 CD: Philips 446 5362

Overture in the Italian style D591

Dresden 1966	Dresden Staatskapelle	LP: Philips SBAL 40/SAL 3672/6747 491 CD: Philips 446 5362

Die Zwillingsbrüder

Munich	Bavarian State	LP: EMI 1C 065 28833/1C 151 53043-53045
January 1975	Orchestra & Chorus	Excerpts
	Donath, Gedda,	LP: EMI EX 29 04323
	Fischer-Dieskau,	
	Moll	

6 Antiphons for Palm Sunday D696

Munich	Bavarian Radio	LP: EMI SLS 5254
February 1982	Chorus	CD: EMI CMS 764 7832

Auguste jam coelestium D48

Munich	Bavarian RO	LP: EMI SLS 5254
February 1982	Popp, Dallapozza	CD: EMI CMS 764 7832

Deutsche Messe D872

Munich	Bavarian Radio	LP: EMI SLS 5254
February 1982	Orchestra & Chorus	LP: EMI CMS 764 7832/CDZ 568 0632

Deutsches Salve regina for organ and chorus D379

Munich	Bavarian Radio	LP: EMI SLS 5254
February 1982	Chorus	CD: EMI CMS 764 7782
	Schloter	

Gesang der Geister über den Wassern D714

Munich	Bavarian Radio	LP: EMI 1C 039 143 2541
1980	Orchestra & Chorus	

Gradual D184

Munich	Bavarian Radio	LP: EMI SLS 5254
September 1980	Orchestra & Chorus	CD: EMI CMS 764 7832

Hymnus an den Heiligen Geist D964

Munich June 1979	Bavarian Radio Orchestra Capella Bavariae	LP: EMI SLS 143 6073 CD: EMI CMS 764 7832

Kyrie in D minor K31

Munich March and December 1981	Bavarian Radio Orchestra & Chorus Popp, Dallapozza	LP: EMI SLS 5254 CD: EMI CMS 764 7832

Kyrie in B flat D45

Munich February 1982	Bavarian Radio Chorus	LP: EMI SLS 5254 CD: EMI CMS 764 7782

Kyrie in D minor D49

Munich March and December 1981	Bavarian Radio Orchestra & Chorus Popp, Fassbaender, Dallapozza, Fischer-Dieskau	LP: EMI SLS 5254 CD: EMI CMS 764 7782

Kyrie in F D66

Munich January– February 1980	Bavarian Radio Orchestra & Chorus	LP: EMI SLS 5278 CD: EMI CMS 764 7832

Lazarus, oratorio D689

Munich June 1983	Bavarian Radio Orchestra & Chorus Donath, Popp, Venuti, Protschka, Tear, Fischer-Dieskau	LP: EMI SLS 143 6073 CD: EMI CMS 764 7832 <u>Excerpt</u> LP: EMI EX 29 04353

Magnificat in C D486

Munich March and December 1981	Bavarian Radio Orchestra & Chorus Popp, Fassbaender, Dallapozza, Fischer-Dieskau	LP: EMI SLS 143 6073 CD: EMI CMS 764 7832

Mass No 1 D105

Munich March and December 1981	Bavarian Radio Orchestra & Chorus Popp, Donath, Fassbaender, Dallapozza, Schreier, Fischer-Dieskau	LP: EMI SLS 5254 CD: EMI CMS 764 7782

Mass No 2 D167

Munich March and December 1981	Bavarian Radio Orchestra & Chorus Popp, Dallapozza, Fischer-Dieskau	LP: EMI SLS 5278 CD: EMI CMS 764 7782 .

Mass No 3 D324

Munich December 1981	Bavarian Radio Orchestra & Chorus Popp, Fassbaender, Dallapozza, Fischer-Dieskau	LP: EMI SLS 5254 CD: EMI CMS 764 7782

Mass No 4 D452

Munich March and December 1981	Bavarian Radio Orchestra & Chorus Popp, Fassbaender, Dallapozza, Fischer-Dieskau	LP: EMI SLS 5278 CD: EMI CDM 769 2222/CMS 764 7782 CD: EMI CZS 767 8622/CMS 565 8422

Mass No 5 D678

Dresden June 1971	Dresden Staatskapelle Leipzig Radio Chorus Donath, Springer, Schreier, Adam	LP: Philips 6500 329 CD: Philips 426 6542
Munich January 1980	Bavarian Radio Orchestra & Chorus Donath, Fassbaender,Araiza, Fischer-Dieskau	LP: EMI SLS 143 6073 CD: EMI CDM 769 2222/CMS 764 7782 CD: EMI CZS 767 8622

Mass No 6 D950

Dresden June 1971	Dresden Staatskapelle Leipzig Radio Chorus Donath, Springer, Schreier, Rotzsch, Adam	LP: Philips 6500 330/416 8621 CD: Philips 426 6542
Munich September 1980	Bavarian Radio Orchestra & Chorus Donath, Fassbaender, Araiza, Fischer-Dieskau	LP: EMI SLS 5278 CD: EMI CMS 764 7782

Nachtgesang im Walde D913

Munich 1980	Capella Bavariae	LP: EMI 1C 039 143 2541

Offertorium in C D136

Munich June 1983	Bavarian Radio Orchestra Donath	LP: EMI SLS 143 6073 CD: EMI CMS 764 7832

Offertorium in A minor D181

Munich January- February 1980	Bavarian Radio Orchestra & Chorus	LP: EMI SLS 143 6073 CD: EMI CMS 764 7832

Offertorium in B flat D963

Munich	Bavarian Radio	LP: EMI SLS 143 6073
September 1980	Orchestra & Chorus	CD: EMI CMS 764 7782
	Schreier	

Psalm 23 D706

Munich	Capella Bavariae	LP: EMI SLS 5278
October 1977	Sawallisch, piano	CD: EMI CMS 764 7832

Psalm 92 D953

Munich	Capella Bavariae	LP: EMI ASD 4415/1C 067 43383
November 1977	Fischer-Dieskau	CD: EMI CDC 747 4072/CMS 764 7832

Salve regina in B flat D106

Munich	Bavarian RO	LP: EMI SLS 5254
January-	Araiza	CD: EMI CMS 764 7832
February 1980		

Salve regina in F D223

Munich	Bavarian RO	LP: EMI SLS 143 6073
June 1983	Donath	CD: EMI CMS 764 7832

Salve regina in B flat D386

Munich	Bavarian Radio	LP: EMI SLS 5254
February 1982	Chorus	CD: EMI CMS 764 7782

Salve regina in A D676

Munich	Bavarian RO	LP: EMI SLS 143 6073
June 1983	Donath	CD: EMI CMS 764 7832

Salve regina in C D811

Munich	Capella Bavariae	LP: EMI SLS 143 6073
June 1983		CD: EMI CMS 764 7832

Stabat mater D175

Munich March and December 1981	Bavarian Radio Orchestra & Chorus	LP: EMI SLS 5254 CD: EMI CMS 764 7832/CMS 565 8452

Stabat mater D383

Munich June 1983	Bavarian Radio Orchestra & Chorus Donath, Protschka, Fischer-Dieskau	LP: EMI SLS 143 6073 CD: EMI CMS 764 7782/CMS 565 8452 Excerpt LP: EMI EX 29 04353

Tantum ergo D460

Munich February 1982	Bavarian Radio Orchestra & Chorus Rüggeberg	LP: EMI SLS 5278 CD: EMI CMS 764 7832

Tantum ergo D461

Munich February 1982	Bavarian Radio Orchestra & Chorus Rüggeberg, Falk, Gassner, Lika	LP: EMI SLS 5278 CD: EMI CMS 764 7832

Tantum ergo D739

Munich January- February 1980	Bavarian Radio Orchestra & Chorus	LP: EMI SLS 5278 CD: EMI CMS 764 7832

Tantum ergo D750

Munich January- February 1980	Bavarian Radio Orchestra & Chorus	LP: EMI SLS 5278 CD: EMI CMS 764 7832

Tantum ergo D962

Munich December 1981	Bavarian Radio Orchestra & Chorus Popp, Fassbaender, Dallapozza, Fischer-Dieskau	LP: EMI SLS 5254 CD: EMI CMS 764 7782

Trinklied D75

Munich June 1983	Capella Bavariae Fischer-Dieskau Sawallisch, piano	LP: EMI SLS 5220/1C 039 143 2541

Zur guten Nacht D903

Munich June 1983	Capella Bavariae Fischer-Dieskau Sawallisch, piano	LP: EMI SLS 5220/1C 039 143 2541

ROBERT SCHUMANN (1810-1856)

Symphony No 1 "Spring"

Dresden September 1972	Dresden Staatskapelle	LP: EMI SLS 867/SXLP 30526 CD: EMI CDM 769 4712/CMS 764 8152

Symphony No 2

Dresden September 1972	Dresden Staatskapelle	LP: EMI SLS 867 CD: EMI CDM 769 4722/CMS 764 8152

Symphony No 3 "Rhenish"

Dresden September 1972	Dresden Staatskapelle	LP: EMI SLS 867 CD: EMI CDM 769 4722/CMS 764 8152

Symphony No 4

Dresden September 1972	Dresden Staatskapelle	LP: EMI SLS 867/SXLP 30526 CD: EMI CDM 769 4712/CMS 764 8152

Overture, Scherzo and Finale

Dresden	Dresden	LP: EMI SLS 867
September 1972	Staatskapelle	CD: EMI CDM 769 4712/CDZ 568 0632

Szenen aus Goethes Faust: Excerpts (Des Lebens Pulse schlagen frisch; Die Nacht scheint tiefer hereinzudringen; Ein Sumpf zieht am Gebirge hin)

Salzburg	VPO	CD: Orfeo C336 931B
July 1961	Fischer-Dieskau	

Mass in C minor

Berlin	BPO	CD: EMI CDC 749 7632
September 1987	Düsseldorf Choir	
	Shirai, Seiffert,	
	Rootering	

Requiem

Munich	Bavarian Radio	CD: RCA/BMG RD 69001
1984	Orchestra & Chorus	
	Donath, Lipovsek,	
	T.Moser, Rootering	

Requiem für Mignon

Munich	Bavarian Radio	CD: RCA/BMG RD 69001
1984	Orchestra & Chorus	
	Kaufmann, Calm,	
	T.Moser, Rootering	

BEDRICH SMETANA (1824-1884)

Ma Vlast

Geneva	Suisse Romande	CD: RCA/BMG RD 83242
December 1977	Orchestra	

JOHANN STRAUSS I (1804-1849)

Radetzky March

Bregenz August 1967	VSO	CD: Orfeo C236 901B

JOHANN STRAUSS II (1825-1899)

Accelerations, waltz

Vienna 1959	VSO	LP: Philips GL 5871/SGL 5871 LP: Philips 6530 010/6747 041/6747 051

Annen Polka

Bregenz August 1967	VSO	CD: Orfeo C236 901B

An der schönen blauen Donau, waltz

Vienna 1959	VSO	LP: Philips G03116L/837 021GY/6530 010 LP: Philips GL 5793/SFL 14115/6747 051 CD: Philips 434 5422

Auf der Jagd, polka

Vienna 1959	VSO	LP: Philips GL 5871/SGL 5871 LP: Philips 6747 041/6747 051
Bregenz August 1967	VSO	CD: Orfeo C236 901B

Die Fledermaus, Overture

Bregenz August 1967	VSO	CD: Orfeo C236 901B

Frühlingsstimmen, waltz

Vienna	VSO	LP: Philips G03116L/837 021GY
1959		LP: Philips GL 5793/SFL 14115
		LP: Philips 6747 041/6747 051
		CD: Philips 434 5422

G'schichten aus dem Wienerwald, waltz

Bregenz	VSO	CD: Orfeo C236 901B
August 1967		

Kaiserwalzer

Vienna	VSO	LP: Philips G03116L/837 021GY
1959		LP: Philips 6527 157/6747 041/6747 051
		CD: Philips 434 5422

Künstlerleben, waltz

Vienna	VSO	LP: Philips G03116L/837 021GY
1959		LP: Philips GL 5793/SFL 14115
		LP: Philips 6747 041/6747 051
		CD: Philips 434 5422

Morgenblätter, waltz

Vienna	VSO	LP: Philips GL 5871/SGL 5871
1959		LP: Philips 6747 041/6747 051

Neue Pizzicato Polka

Vienna	VSO	LP: Philips GL 5871/SGL 5871
1959		LP: Philips 6530 010/6747 041/6747 051

Perpetuum mobile

Vienna	VSO	LP: Philips GL 5871/SGL 5871
1959		LP: Philips 6747 041/6747 051

Rosen aus dem Süden, waltz

Vienna   VSO   LP: Philips G03116L/837 021GY
1959   LP: Philips GL 5793/SFL 14115
                          LP: Philips 6530 010/6747 041/6747 051
                          CD: Philips 434 5422

Tik-Tak Polka

Vienna   VSO   LP: Philips GL 5871/SGL 5871
1959   LP: Philips 6530 010/6747 041/6747 051

Tritsch-Tratsch Polka

Vienna   VSO   LP: Philips GL 5871/SGL 5871
1959   LP: Philips 6530 010/6747 041/6747 051

Unter Donner und Blitz, polka

Vienna   VSO   LP: Philips GL 5871/SGL 5871
1959   LP: Philips 6747 041/6747 051

Wein Weib und Gesang, waltz

Vienna   VSO   LP: Philips G03116L/837 021GY
1959   LP: Philips GL 5793/SFL 14115
                          LP: Philips 6530 010/6747 041/6747 051
                          CD: Philips 434 5422

Wiener Bonbons, waltz

Vienna   VSO   LP: Philips GL 5871/SGL 5871
1959   LP: Philips 6530 010/6747 041/6747 051

Wo die Zitronen blüh'n, waltz

Vienna   VSO   LP: Philips GL 5871/SGL 5871
1959   LP: Philips 6747 041/6747 051

JOSEF STRAUSS (1827-1870)

Auf Ferienreisen, polka

Bregenz August 1967	VSO	CD: Orfeo C236 901B

Feuerfest, polka

Bregenz August 1967	VSO	CD: Orfeo C236 901B

Jockey Polka

Bregenz August 1967	VSO	CD: Orfeo C236 901B

Plappermäulchen, polka

Bregenz August 1967	VSO	CD: Orfeo C236 901B

RICHARD STRAUSS (1864-1949)

Arabella

Munich July 1980	Bavarian State Orchestra & Chorus Varady, Donath, Dallapozza, Berry, Fischer-Dieskau	LP: EMI SLS 5220/1C 165 64456-64458 LP: Angel 3917 LP: Orfeo S169 882H CD: Orfeo C169 882H

Capriccio

London September 1957	Philharmonia Schwarzkopf, Moffo, C.Ludwig, Gedda, Fischer-Dieskau, Hotter, Wächter, Schmitt-Walter	LP: Columbia 33CX 1600-1602 LP: Columbia (Germany) C 90997-90999 LP: Angel 3580 LP: World Records OC 230-232 LP: EMI 143 5243 CD: EMI CDS 749 0148 Excerpts LP: World Records OH 223 CD: EMI CDM 763 6572/CMS 763 7902 CD: EMI CDZ 568 0632

Elektra

Munich June 1990	Bavarian Radio Orchestra & Chorus Marton, Studer, Lipovsek, Winkler, Weikl	CD: EMI CDS 754 0672

Die Frau ohne Schatten

Munich September 1976	Bavarian State Orchestra & Chorus Nilsson, Bjoner, Varnay, King, Fischer-Dieskau	CD: Legendary LRCD 1029 Also issued on LP by Legendary
Munich February- December 1987	Bavarian Radio Orchestra & Chorus Studer, H.Schwarz, Vintzing, Kollo, Muff	CD: EMI CDS 749 0742 Excerpts CD: EMI CDC 754 4942

Intermezzo

Munich January 1980	Bavarian RO Popp, Dallapozza, Fischer-Dieskau, Moll	LP: EMI SLS 5204/1C 165 30983-30985 CD: EMI CDS 749 3372 Excerpt LP: EMI EX 29 04323

Intermezzo, Waltz scene

London March 1958	Philharmonia	LP: Columbia 33CX 1647 LP: Angel 35646

Die schweigsame Frau

Munich 1973	Bavarian State Orchestra & Chorus Grist, Mödl, Grobe, McDaniel, Moll, Kusche	Unpublished video recording

Also sprach Zarathustra

Philadelphia 1995	Philadelphia Orchestra	CD: EMI awaiting publication

Le bougeois gentilhomme, Suite of incidental music

London February-March 1958	Philharmonia	LP: Columbia 33CX 1647 LP: Angel 35646

Burleske for piano and orchestra

Philadelphia 1995	Philadelphia Orchestra Ax	CD: EMI awaiting publication

Don Juan

Philadelphia 1995	Philadelphia Orchestra	CD: EMI awaiting publication

Festliches Präludium

Tokyo May 1993	Philadelphia Orchestra	CD: EMI CDC 555 1852

Ein Heldenleben

Philadelphia 1994-1995	Philadelphia Orchestra	EMI awaiting publication

Horn Concerto No 1

London September 1956	Philharmonia Brain	LP: Columbia 33CX 1491 LP: Columbia (Germany) C 90565 LP: EMI HLS 7001/RLS 7701 CD: EMI CDC 747 8342

Horn Concerto No 2

London	Philharmonia	LP: Columbia 33CX 1491
September 1956	Brain	LP: Columbia (Germany) C 90565
		LP: EMI HLS 7001/RLS 7701
		CD: EMI CDC 747 8342

Oboe Concerto

Philadelphia	Philadelphia	EMI awaiting publication
1994-1995	Orchestra	
	Woodhams	

4 letzte Lieder

Philadelphia	Philadelphia	CD: EMI CDC 555 5942
September-	Orchestra	
October 1994	Hendricks	

Sinfonia domestica

Tokyo	Philadelphia	CD: EMI CDC 555 1852
May 1993	Orchestra	

Till Eulenspiegels lustige Streiche

Tokyo	Philadelphia	CD: EMI CDC 555 1852
May 1993	Orchestra	

Sonatina in E flat "Fröhliche Werkstatt"

Munich	Munich Wind	CD: Orfeo C004 821A
1982	Academy	

Songs with orchestra: Ich wollt' ein Sträusslein binden; Säusle liebe Myrthe

Philadelphia	Philadelphia	CD: EMI CDC 555 5942
September-	Orchestra	
October 1994	Hendricks	

PIOTR TCHAIKOVSKY (1840-1893)

Symphony No 5

Amsterdam January 1962	Concertgebouw Orchestra	LP: Philips A02228L/835 116AY

Piano Concerto No 1

Berlin 1953	Berlin RO Hansen	LP: Remington

The Nutcracker, Suite

London September 1957	Philharmonia	LP: Columbia 33CX 1623/SAX 2285 LP: Angel 35644 LP: EMI CFP 40002 CD: Royal Classics ROY 6460 Excerpts 45: Columbia SEL 1628

Swan Lake, ballet

Philadelphia October 1993- May 1994	Philadelphia Orchestra	CD: EMI CDS 555 2772

Swan Lake, Suite

London September and October 1957 and February 1958	Philharmonia	LP: Columbia 33CX 1623/SAX 2285 LP: Angel 35644 LP: EMI CFP 40002 CD: Royal Classics ROY 6460 Excerpts 45: Columbia SEL 1628

Transcriptions by Stokowski: 1.Andante cantabile; 2.At the ball

Collingswood NJ March 1995	Philadelphia Orchestra Lipovsek (2)	CD: EMI CDC 555 5922

GIUSEPPE VERDI (1813-1901)

La Forza del destino, Overture

Munich 1984	Bavarian State Orchestra	CD: Orfeo C161 871A

Macbeth

Salzburg August 1964	VPO Vienna Opera Chorus Bumbry, Lorenzi, Fischer-Dieskau, Lagger	CD: Frequenz 011.036 Excerpts CD: Orfeo C335 931A

RICHARD WAGNER (1813-1883)

Die Feen

Munich July 1983	Bavarian State Orchestra & Chorus Gray, Lövaas, Laki, Anderson, Studer, Alexander, Orth, R.Hermann, Moll, Rootering	LP: Orfeo S062 833F CD: Orfeo C062 833F

Der fliegende Holländer

Bayreuth July 1959	Bayreuth Festival Orchestra & Chorus Rysanek, Fischer, Uhl, London, Greindl	LP: Melodram MEL 590 CD: Melodram MEL 26101 Excerpts LP: Rodolphe RP 12433-12434 LP: Melodram MEL 650 CD: Myto MCD 89002
Bayreuth August 1961	Bayreuth Festival Orchestra & Chorus Silja, Fischer, Uhl, Crass, Greindl	LP: Philips A02211-02213L/835 104-106AY LP: Philips SABL 218-220/6723 001/6747 248 CD: Philips 442 1032 Excerpts LP: Philips 6527 108/412 0241
Milan February 1966	La Scala Orchestra and Chorus Rysanek, Bessel, Heater, Crass, Ridderbusch	CD: Memories HR 4281-4282
Munich February- March 1991	Bavarian State Orchestra & Chorus Varady, Schlemm, Seiffert, Hale, Ryhänen	VHS Video: EMI MVD 991 3113 Laserdisc: EMI LDC 991 3111

A Faust Overture

Philadelphia 1994-1995	Philadelphia Orchestra	EMI awaiting publication

Der fliegende Holländer, Overture

Vienna November 1959	VSO	LP: Philips ABL 3404/SABL 210 LP: Philips SFM 23005/6580 063 CD: Philips 422 4802/434 5462

Götterdämmerung

Munich November 1989	Bavarian State Orchestra & Chorus Behrens, Balslev, Meier, Kollo, Nöcker, Salminen, Wlaschiha	VHS Video: EMI MVB 991 2873 Laserdisc: EMI LDF 991 2871/LDX 991 2751

Götterdämmerung, Siegfried's Rhine Journey and Funeral March

London February 1958	Philharmonia	LP: Columbia 33CX 1655 LP: Angel 35755 CD: EMI CMS 565 2122

Das Liebesverbot

Munich July 1983	Bavarian State Orchestra & Chorus Hass, Coburn, Schunk, Prey, Engen	CD: Orfeo C345 953D

Das Liebesverbot, Overture

Philadelphia 1994-1995	Philadelphia Orchestra	EMI awaiting publication

Lohengrin

Bayreuth July 1962	Bayreuth Festival Orchestra & Chorus Silja, Varnay, Thomas, Vinay, Crass, Krause	LP: Philips 6747 241 CD: Philips 446 3372 <u>Excerpts</u> LP: Philips 6527 108/412 0221
Milan March 1965	La Scala Orchestra and Chorus Bjoner, Varnay, Thomas, Neidlinger, Crass, Krause	CD: Melodram MEL 37067
Munich July 1978	Bavarian State Orchestra & Chorus Ligendza, Randova, Kollo, Roar, Ridderbusch, Brendel	Unpublished radio broadcast

Lohengrin, Preludes Acts 1 and 3

Vienna May 1963	VSO	LP: Philips

Die Meistersinger von Nürnberg

Munich April 1993	Bavarian State Orchestra & Chorus Studer, Kallisch, Heppner, Van der Welt, Weikl, Moll, Lorenz	CD: EMI CDS 555 1422

Die Meistersinger von Nürnberg, Overture

London July 1958	Philharmonia	LP: Columbia 33CX 1655 LP: Angel 35755
Vienna May 1963	VSO	LP: Philips
Munich 1984	Bavarian State Orchestra	CD: Orfeo C161 871A

Die Meistersinger von Nürnberg, Act 3 Prelude

Vienna May 1963	VSO	LP: Philips

Parsifal, Prelude and Karfreitagszauber

Vienna May 1963	VSO	LP: Philips

Das Rheingold

Munich November 1989	Bavarian State Orchestra Gustafson, Lipovsek, Schwarz, Tear, Pampuch, Hale, Wlaschiha, Moll, Rootering	VHS Video: EMI MVB 991 2763 Laserdisc: EMI LDD 991 2761/LDX 991 2751

Rienzi

Munich July 1983	Bavarian State Orchestra & Chorus Studer, Kollo, Janssen, Rootering, Brinkmann	CD: Orfeo C346 953D

Rienzi, Overture

Vienna November 1959	VSO	LP: Philips ABL 3404/SABL 210 LP: Philips SFM 23005/6580 063/6833 154 CD: Philips 422 4802/434 5462
Philadelphia 1994-1995	Philadelphia Orchestra	EMI awaiting publication

Siegfried

Munich November 1989	Bavarian State Orchestra Behrens, Kaufmann, Schwarz, Kollo, Pampuvh, Hale, Moll, Wlaschiha	VHS Video: EMI MVB 991 2833 Laserdisc: EMI LDE 991 2831/LDX 991 2751

Siegfried Idyll

Vienna April 1960	VSO	LP: Philips ABL 3404/SABL 210 LP: Philips SFM 23005/6580 063 CD: Philips 422 4802/434 5462

Symphony in E

Philadelphia 1994-1995	Philadelphia Orchestra	EMI awaiting publication

Tannhäuser

Bayreuth July 1961	Bayreuth Festival Orchestra & Chorus De los Angeles, Bumbry, Windgassen, Stolze, Greindl, Fischer-Dieskau, Crass	LP: Ed Smith UORC 230 LP: Melodram MEL 614 CD: Myto MCD 93277 Also published on LP by Teatro Dischi
Bayreuth July and August 1962 *Wachter*	Bayreuth Festival Orchestra & Chorus Silja, Bumbry, Windgassen, Stolze, ~~Fischer-Dieskau~~, Greindl, Crass	LP: Philips SAL 3445-3447/835 178-180AY LP: Philips 6723 001/6747 242 LP: Philips 6747 249/6770 026 CD: Philips 420 1222/434 4202/434 6072 Excerpts LP: Philips 6527 108/412 0231/446 6202
Milan April 1967	La Scala Orchestra and Chorus Jurinac, Martin, Beirer, Morris, Braun, Talvela	CD: Melodram CDM 37091
Perugia October 1972	Orchestra & Chorus Janowitz, Dunn, Kollo, Brendel, Schenk	Unpublished radio broadcast

Tannhäuser, Overture

London July 1958	Philharmonia	LP: Columbia 33CX 1655 LP: Angel 35755

Tannhäuser, Venusberg music

Vienna January 1961	VSO	LP: Philips ABL 3404/SABL 210 LP: Philips SFM 23005/6580 063 CD: Philips 422 4802/434 5462

Tristan und Isolde

Bayreuth July 1957	Bayreuth Festival Orchestra & Chorus Nilsson, G.Hoffman, Windgassen, Hotter, Van Mill	LP: Melodram MEL 575
Munich July 1980	Bavarian State Orchestra & Chorus Behrens, Minton, Wenkoff, Moll, Nimsgern	Unpublished radio broadcast

Die Walküre

Munich November 1989	Bavarian State Orchestra Varady, Behrens, Lipovsek, Schunk, Hale, Moll	VHS Video: EMI MVB 991 2793 Laserdisc: EMI LDE 991 2791/LDX 991 2751

Wesendonk-Lieder, orchestrated by Henze

Collingswood NJ March 1995	Philadelphia Orchestra Lipovsek	EMI awaiting publication

CARL MARIA VON WEBER (1786-1826)

Symphonies Nos 1 and 2

Date not confirmed	Bavarian RO	CD: Orfeo C091 841A

Abu Hassan

Munich 1974	Bavarian State Orchestra Moser, Gedda, Moll	LP: EMI 1C 063 30148

Abu Hassan, Overture

London July 1958	Philharmonia	LP: Columbia 33CX 1652/SAX 2343 LP: Angel 35754 LP: EMI XLP 30038/SXLP 30038/SMVP 8062 CD: EMI CDM 769 5722

Beherrscher der Geister, Overture

London July 1958	Philharmonia	LP: Columbia 33CX 1652/SAX 2343 LP: Angel 35754 LP: EMI XLP 30038/SXLP 30038/SMVP 8062 CD: EMI CDM 769 5722

Euryanthe

Munich July 1986	Bamberg SO Bavarian Radio Chorus Studer, Bjoner, Ramirez, Adam, Schenk	Unpublished radio broadcast

Euryanthe, Overture

London February 1958	Philharmonia	LP: Columbia 33CX 1652/SAX 2343 LP: Angel 35754 LP: EMI XLP 30038/SXLP 30038/SMVP 8062 CD: EMI CDM 769 5722

Der Freischütz

Florence May 1995	Maggio Musicale Orchestra & Chorus Margiono, Kilduff, Seiffert, Wlaschiha, Surjan, Trajanov	Unpublished radio broadcast

Der Freischütz, Overture

London February 1958	Philharmonia	LP: Columbia 33CX 1652/SAX 2343 LP: Angel 35754 LP: EMI XLP 30038/SXLP 30038/SMVP 8062

Jubel, Overture

London July 1958	Philharmonia	LP: Columbia 33CX 1652/SAX 2343 LP: Angel 35754 LP: EMI XLP 30038/SXLP 30038/SMVP 8062 CD: EMI CDM 769 5722

Oberon, Overture

London February– July 1958	Philharmonia	LP: Columbia 33CX 1652/SAX 2343 LP: Angel 35754 LP: EMI XLP 30038/SXLP 30038/SMVP 8062 CD: EMI CDM 769 5722

Preciosa, Overture

London February 1958	Philharmonia	LP: Columbia 33CX 1652/SAX 2343 LP: Angel 35754 LP: EMI XLP 30038/SXLP 30038/SMVP 8062 CD: EMI CDM 763 5722

WOLFGANG SAWALLISCH AS PIANIST

JOHANN SEBASTIAN BACH (1685-1750)

Concerto for 4 pianos BWV1065

Munich 1972	Bavarian RO Sawallisch, 4th piano Kempe & Rieger, 1st and 3rd pianos, Kubelik conducting from 2nd piano	CD: Hunt CDMP 4941

JOHANNES BRAHMS (1833-1897)

94 Lieder

Salzburg August 1973	Fischer-Dieskau	LP: EMI SLS 5002/1C 191 50379-50385 CD: EMI CMS 764 8202

Liebeslieder-Walzer and Neue Liebeslieder-Walzer

Berlin September 1981	Mathis, Fassbaender, Schreier, Fischer-Dieskau Engel & Sawallisch, pianos	LP: DG 2740 280/2532 094 CD: DG 423 1332

Vocal duets and quartets

Berlin September 1981	Mathis, Fassbaender, Schreier, Fischer-Dieskau Engel & Sawallisch, pianos	LP: DG 2740 280 LP: DG 2532 094 (selection) CD: DG 423 1332 (selection)

Horn Trio

1995	Neunecker, horn Zimmermann, violin Sawallisch, piano	EMI awaiting publication

FRANZ DANZI (1763-1826)

Wind Quintet in D minor

Munich 1985	Munich Residenz Quartet	CD: Claves CD 50 8101

GABRIEL FAURE (1845-1924)

La bonne chanson, song cycle

Berlin 1975	Fischer-Dieskau	LP: BASF 22 7650

GUSTAV MAHLER (1860-1911)

Lieder aus Des Knaben Wunderhorn

Salzburg August 1976	Fischer-Dieskau	CD: Orfeo C333 931B/C339 930T

FELIX MENDELSSOHN-BARTHOLDY (1809-1847)

3 Eichendorff-Lieder

Salzburg August 1975	Fischer-Dieskau	CD: Orfeo C185 891A/C339 930T

40 Lieder

Berlin September 1970	Fischer-Dieskau	LP: EMI SLS 805/1C 157 02180-02181 LP: EMI EX 29 04292 (selection) CD: EMI CMS 764 8272

HANS PFITZNER (1869-1949)

6 Eichendorff-Lieder

Salzburg August 1975	Fischer-Dieskau	CD: Orfeo C185 891A/C339 930T

MAURICE RAVEL (1875-1937)

3 chansons madécasses

Berlin 1975	Fischer-Dieskau Zöller, flute Böttcher, cello	LP: BASF 22 7650

NIKOLAI RIMSKY-KORSAKOV (1844-1908)

Quintet for piano and wind instruments

Munich 1983	Munich Residenz Quartet	CD: Calig CAL 50898

ANTON RUBINSTEIN (1829-1894)

Quintet for piano and wind instruments

Munich 1983	Munich Residenz Quartet	CD: Calig CAL 50898

FRANZ SCHUBERT (1797-1828)

12 Lieder

Munich 1980	M.Price	CD: Orfeo C001 811A

Winterreise

Munich October 1971	Prey	LP: Philips 6747 033/6747 059 CD: Philips 422 9392/422 2422/442 6922

Der Gondelfahrer D809

Munich 1980	Capella Bavariae	LP: EMI 1C 039 143 2541

Mirjams Siegesgesang D 942

Munich 1980	Capella Bavariae Behrens, Rüggeberg, Greindl-Rosner, Heutersmann, Falk	LP: EMI 1C 039 143 2541

Mondenschein D875

Munich 1980	Capella Bavariae Schreier	LP: EMI 1C 039 143 2541

Nachthelle D892

Munich 1980	Capella Bavariae Schreier	LP: EMI 1C 039 143 2541

Ständchen D92

Munich 1980	Capella Bavariae Fassbaender	LP: EMI 1C 039 143 2541

ROBERT SCHUMANN (1810-1856)

6 Eichendorff-Lieder

Salzburg August 1975	Fischer-Dieskau	CD: Orfeo C185 891A/C339 930T

Lieder

1994-1995	Hampson	EMI awaiting publication

REINHARD SCHWARZ-SCHILLING (1904-1987)

3 Eichendorff-Lieder

Salzburg August 1975	Fischer-Dieskau	CD: Orfeo C185 891A/C339 930T

LUDWIG SPOHR (1784-1859)

Quintet for piano and wind instruments

Munich 1985	Munich Residenz Quartet	CD: Claves CD 50 8101

RICHARD STRAUSS (1864-1949)

49 Lieder

Munich and Berlin October 1981- September 1985	Fischer-Dieskau	LP: DG 413 4551 LP: DG 415 4701 (selection) CD: DG 447 5122 CD: DG 415 4702 (selection)

17 Lieder

Munich April and May 1986	M.Price	CD: EMI CDC 747 9482

21 Lieder

Munich September 1984	Popp	CD: EMI CDC 749 3182

13 Lieder

Munich September 1995	Hendricks	CD: EMI CDC 555 5942 <u>CD also includes 4 letzte Lieder and 2 other songs with orchestra: see main discography</u>

BRUNO WALTER (1876-1962)

2 Eichendorff-Lieder

Salzburg August 1975	Fischer-Dieskau	CD: Orfeo C185 891A/C339 930T

HUGO WOLF (1860-1903)

21 Goethe-Lieder

Munich	Schreier	LP: Eurodisc 610 098.231
October 1981		CD: RCA/Eurodisc GD 69117

7 Eichendorff-Lieder

Salzburg	Fischer-Dieskau	CD: Orfeo C185 891A/C339 930T
August 1975		

<u>Full contents of the recorded recitals with Dietrich Fischer-Dieskau can be found in the discography "A Notable Quartet", compiled by John Hunt in 1995 (ISBN 0 9525827 1 6).</u>

Rafael Kubelik
born 1914

Discography compiled by John Hunt

JOHANN SEBASTIAN BACH (1685-1750)

Concerto for 4 pianos BWV 1065

Munich 1972	Bavarian RO Kubelik conducting from 2nd piano, Kempe, Rieger and Sawallisch, 1st, 3rd and 4th pianos	CD: Hunt CDMP 4941

Violin Concerto in E BWV 1042

London June 1959	LSO de Vito	LP: HMV ALP 1856/ASD 429

BELA BARTOK (1881-1945)

Concerto for orchestra

London April 1958	RPO	LP: HMV ALP 1744/ASD 312 LP: Electrola E 91064/STE 91064 CD: EMI CZS 568 2232
Boston November 1973	Boston SO	LP: DG 2530 479/2535 499/410 9931 CD: DG 437 2742

Music for strings, percussion and celesta

Chicago April 1951	Chicago SO	LP: Mercury MG 50001 LP: HMV BLP 1032

2 Portraits

London June 1958	RPO	LP: HMV ALP 1744/ASD 312 LP: Electrola E 91064/STE 91064

LUDWIG VAN BEETHOVEN (1770-1827)

Symphony No 1

London June 1974	LSO	LP: DG 2740 155

Symphony No 2

Amsterdam February 1974	Concertgebouw Orchestra	LP: DG 2740 155

Symphony No 3 "Eroica"

Berlin October 1971	BPO	LP: DG 2740 155/2535 412 CD: Belart 450 0372

Symphony No 4

Tel Aviv September 1975	Israel PO	LP: DG 2740 155

Symphony No 5

Boston November 1973	Boston SO	LP: DG 2740 155 CD: Belart 450 0382

Symphony No 6 "Pastoral"

London January 1959	RPO	LP: HMV ALP 1771/ASD 349/SIT 60039
Munich 1972	Bavarian RO	CD: Originals SH 848
Paris January 1973	Orchestre de Paris	LP: DG 2740 155

Symphony No 7

Munich March- April 1970	Bavarian RO	LP: DG 2535 252
Vienna September 1974	VPO	LP: DG 2740 155 CD: Belart 450 0382

Symphony No 8

Cleveland March 1975	Cleveland Orchestra	LP: DG 2740 155/2727 010

Symphony No 9 "Choral"

Munich January 1975	Bavarian Radio Orchestra & Chorus Donath, Berganza, Ochman, Stewart	LP: DG 2740 155/2727 010
Munich 1982	Bavarian Radio Orchestra & Chorus Donath, Fassbaender, Laubenthal, Sotin	CD: Orfeo C207 891B

Piano Concerto No 1

London October 1948	Philharmonia Gieseking	78: Columbia LX 1312-15/8732-35 auto 78: Columbia (Germany) LWX 394-397 78: Columbia (France) LFX 983-986 LP: Columbia (USA) ML 4307 LP: Columbia (Germany) C 91244 LP: Columbia (France) FCX 109 LP: EMI 3C 153 52425-52431M <u>Conductor not named on this recording as he was an HMV artist at the time</u>
Date not confirmed	Bavarian RO Serkin	CD: Artists' Live Recordings FED 067
Munich March 1968	Bavarian RO Anda	CD: Orfeo C271 921B

Piano Concerto No 2

Date not confirmed	Bavarian RO Serkin	CD: Artists' Live Recordings FED 067

Piano Concerto No 4

Munich March 1970	Bavarian RO Kempff	Unpublished video recording
Munich 1970	Bavarian RO Brendel	CD: Hunt CDMP 4941

Piano Concerto No 5 "Emperor"

Date not confirmed	Bavarian RO Curzon	CD: Originals SH 800

Violin Concerto

London September 1949	Philharmonia Haendel	78: HMV C 4126-4131/C 7979-7984 auto 45: Victor WBC 1003 LP: Victor LBC 1003 LP: Pathé FALP 138 LP: Toshiba EAC 60235 CD: Testament SBT 1083

Missa Solemnis

Munich March 1977	Bavarian Radio Orchestra & Chorus Donath, Fassbaender, Schreier, Shirley-Quirk	CD: Orfeo C370 942B

Grosse Fuge

Munich 1975	Bavarian RO	CD: Originals SH 838

ALBAN BERG (1885-1935)

Violin Concerto

Munich May 1968	Bavarian RO Szeryng	LP: DG 2530 033 CD: DG 431 7402

HECTOR BERLIOZ (1803-1869)

Les Troyens

New York March 1974	Metropolitan Opera Orchestra & Chorus Verrett, C.Ludwig, Dunn, Vickers, Quilico, Macurdy	Unpublished Met broadcast

Les Troyens, extracts

Milan May 1960	La Scala Orchestra and Chorus Rankin, Simionato, Cossotto, del Monaco, Zaccaria	CD: VAI Audio VAIA 1026

Les Troyens: Excerpt (Je vais mourir)

London 1968	Covent Garden Orchestra Veasey	LP: Decca MET 392-393/SET 392-393

Le carnaval romain, Overture

Munich 1975	Bavarian RO	CD: Originals SH 843

ERNEST BLOCH (1880-1959)

Concerto grosso for strings

Chicago April 1951	Chicago SO	LP: Mercury MG 50001 LP: Mercury Wing MGW 14034/SRW 18034

ALEXANDER BORODIN (1833-1887)

Symphony No 2

Vienna January 1960	VPO	LP: HMV ALP 1848/ASD 422 CD: EMI CZS 568 2232 CD: Toshiba Shinseido SGR 8008

Polovtsian Dances

Vienna January 1960	VPO Wiener Singverein	LP: HMV ALP 1848/ASD 422 CD: Toshiba Shinseido SGR 8008

JOHANNES BRAHMS (1833-1897)

Symphony No 1

Chicago April 1952	Chicago SO	LP: Mercury MG 50007 LP: Mercury Wing MGW 14023/SRW 18023 LP: Philips Wing WL 1016
Vienna September 1957	VPO	LP: Decca LXT 5417/SXL 2013 LP: Decca ADD 117/SDD 117
Munich April 1983	Bavarian RO	CD: Orfeo C070 833D

Symphony No 2

London September 1951	Philharmonia	HMV unpublished
Vienna February- March 1957	VPO	LP: Decca LXT 5339/SXL 2059 LP: Decca ADD 118/SDD 118
Munich April 1983	Bavarian RO	CD: Orfeo C070 833D

Symphony No 3

Vienna September 1957	VPO	LP: Decca LXT 5419/SXL 2104 LP: Decca ADD 119/SDD 119
Munich May 1983	Bavarian RO	CD: Orfeo C070 833D

Symphony No 4

Vienna March 1956	VPO	LP: Decca LXT 5214/SXL 2206 LP: Decca ADD 120/SDD 120
Munich May 1983	Bavarian RO	CD: Orfeo C070 833D

Piano Concerto No 1

London September 1952	Philharmonia Solomon	45: Victor WHMV 1042 LP: HMV ALP 1172 LP: Electrola E 90085 LP: Victor LHMV 1042 LP: Turnabout THS 65110 LP: EMI SLS 5094 CD: Testament SBT 1041

Piano Concerto No 2

Munich October 1962	Bavarian RO Anda	CD: Orfeo C271 921B

Hungarian Dance No 1 in G minor

London November 1958	RPO	45: HMV 7ER 5182/RES 4278 LP: HMV ALP 1769/ASD 347 LP: Electrola E 70393/STE 70393 CD: EMI CDZ 762 6082

Hungarian Dance No 3 in F

London November 1958	RPO	45: HMV 7ER 5182/RES 4278 LP: HMV ALP 1769/ASD 347 LP: Electrola E 70393/STE 70393 CD: EMI CDZ 762 6082

Hungarian Dance No 5 in G minor

London	RPO	45: HMV 7ER 5182/RES 4278
November 1958		LP: HMV ALP 1769/ASD 347
		LP: Electrola E 70393/STE 70393
		CD: EMI CDZ 762 6082

Hungarian Dance No 6 in D

London	RPO	45: HMV 7ER 5182/RES 4278
January 1959		LP: HMV ALP 1769/ASD 347
		LP: Electrola E 70393/STE 70393
		CD: EMI CDZ 762 6082

Hungarian Dance No 7 in F

London	RPO	HMV unpublished
November 1958		

Hungarian Dance No 17 in F sharp minor

London	RPO	45: HMV 7ER 5182/RES 4278
January 1959		LP: HMV ALP 1769/ASD 347
		LP: Electrola E 70393/STE 70393
		CD: EMI CDZ 762 6082/CZS 568 2232

Hungarian Dance No 18 in D

London	RPO	LP: HMV ALP 1769/ASD 347
January 1959		LP: Electrola E 70393/STE 70393
		CD: EMI CDZ 762 6082/CZS 568 2232

Hungarian Dance No 19 in B minor

London	RPO	LP: HMV ALP 1769/ASD 347
January 1959		LP: Electrola E 70393/STE 70393
		CD: EMI CDZ 762 6082/CZS 568 2232

Hungarian Dance No 20 in E minor

London　　　　　RPO　　　　　　　　　LP: HMV ALP 1769/ASD 347
January 1959　　　　　　　　　　　　　LP: Electrola E 70393/STE 70393
　　　　　　　　　　　　　　　　　　　CD: EMI CDZ 762 6082/CZS 565 2232

Hungarian Dance No 21 in E minor

London　　　　　RPO　　　　　　　　　LP: HMV ALP 1769/ASD 347
January 1959　　　　　　　　　　　　　LP: Electrola E 70393/STE 70393
　　　　　　　　　　　　　　　　　　　CD: EMI CDZ 762 6082/CZS 565 2232

MAX BRUCH (1838-1920)

Violin Concerto No 1

London　　　　　Philharmonia　　　　78: HMV C 3802-3804/C 7733-7735 auto
October 1948　　Haendel　　　　　　　45: Victor WBC 1013
　　　　　　　　　　　　　　　　　　　LP: Victor LBC 1013
　　　　　　　　　　　　　　　　　　　CD: Testament SBT 1083

ANTON BRUCKNER (1824-1896)

Symphony No 3

Munich　　　　　Bavarian RO　　　　　CD: Sony MK 39033
October 1980

Symphony No 4 "Romantic"

Munich　　　　　Bavarian RO　　　　　LP: CBS 35914-35915
November 1979　　　　　　　　　　　　CD: Sony MDK 46505

Symphony No 8

Munich　　　　　Bavarian RO　　　　　CD: Orfeo C203 891B
November 1963

FREDERIC CHOPIN (1810-1849)

Piano Concerto No 2

Paris January 1960	Conservatoire Orchestra Haskil	LP: Discocorp RR 233 CD: Disques Montaigne TCE 8780 CD: Seven Seas (Japan) KICC 2371

CLAUDE DEBUSSY (1862-1918)

Pelléas et Mélisande

Munich November 1971	Bavarian RO Donath, Schiml, Gedda, Meven, Fischer-Dieskau	CD: Orfeo C367 942I

ANTONIN DVORAK (1841-1904)

Symphony No 1 "The Bells of Zlonice"

Berlin February 1973	BPO	LP: DG 2720 066/2740 237 CD: DG 423 1202

Symphony No 2

Berlin December 1972	BPO	LP: DG 2720 066/2740 237 CD: DG 423 1202

Symphony No 3

Berlin October 1972	BPO	LP: DG 2720 066/2740 237 CD: DG 423 1202

Symphony No 4

Berlin October 1972	BPO	LP: DG 2720 066/2740 237 CD: DG 423 1202

Symphony No 5

Berlin October 1972	BPO	LP: DG 2720 066/2740 237 CD: DG 423 1202

Symphony No 6

Berlin September 1972	BPO	LP: DG 2720 066/2740 237/2530 425 CD: DG 423 1202

Symphony No 7

London September 1951	Philharmonia	45: Victor WHMV 1029 LP: HMV ALP 1075 LP: Victor LHMV 1029 CD: Testament SBT 1079
Vienna October 1956	VPO	LP: Decca LXT 5290/SXL 2059
Stockholm September 1964	Stockholm PO	CD: Bis BISCD 421-424 Rehearsal of third movement
Berlin January 1971	BPO	LP: DG 2720 066/2740 237/2530 127 CD: DG 423 1202/439 6632/445 0122

Symphony No 8

Prague 1946	Czech PO	CD: Multisonic 31 00192
London October 1948	Philharmonia	78: HMV C 3852-3856/C 7750-7754 auto 45: Victor WHMV 1014 LP: HMV ALP 1064 LP: Victor LHMV 1014 CD: Testament SBT 1079
Tel Aviv April 1957	Israel PO	Decca unpublished
Berlin June 1966	BPO	LP: DG LPM 19 181/SLPM 138 181 LP: DG 2720 066/2740 237/2535 397 CD: DG 423 1202/439 6632 CD: DG 445 0122/447 4122

Symphony No 9 "From the New World"

Chicago 1952	Chicago SO	LP: HMV ALP 1018 LP: Mercury Wing MGW 14021/SRW 18021
Vienna October 1956	VPO	LP: Decca LXT 5291/SXL 2005 LP: Decca ADD 128/SDD 128/ECS 771
Berlin June 1972	BPO	LP: DG 2720 066/2740 237/2530 415 LP: DG 2535 473/2543 513 CD: DG 423 1202/427 2022/439 4362 CD: DG 439 6632/447 4122
Munich 1973	Bavarian RO	CD: Originals SH 838
Prague 1991	Czech PO	CD: Denon CO-79728

Cello Concerto

London October 1948	Philharmonia Fournier	78: HMV DB 6887-6891 CD: Testament SBT 1016
Vienna June 1954	VPO Fournier	LP: Decca LXT 2999/ECS 512

Piano Concerto

Prague 1946	Czech PO Firkusny	CD: Multisonic 31 00192

Serenade for strings

Tel Aviv April 1957	Israel PO	LP: Decca LW 5332/SPA 375
London May 1969	English Chamber Orchestra	LP: DG 139 443/2538 313 CD: DG 445 0372 Excerpt LP: DG 2535 646

Symphonic Variations

Munich June 1974	Bavarian RO	LP: DG 2530 712/2740 238 CD: DG 435 0742

Stabat mater

Munich September 1976	Bavarian Radio Orchestra & Chorus Mathis, Reynolds, Ochman, Shirley-Quirk	LP: DG 2707 099 CD: DG 423 9192

Carnival, Overture

Prague October 1946	Czech PO	78: HMV C 3959/DB 4307
Munich February 1976	Bavarian RO	LP: DG 2530 785/2740 238 CD: DG 423 1202/435 0742

The Golden Spinning Wheel

Munich June 1974	Bavarian RO	LP: DG 2530 713/2740 238 CD: DG 435 0742

Husitska, Overture

Munich February 1976	Bavarian RO	LP: DG 2530 785/2740 238 CD: DG 435 0742

In Nature's Realm, Overture

Prague October 1946	Czech PO	78: HMV C 3628-3629
Munich February 1976	Bavarian RO	LP: DG 2530 785/2740 238 CD: DG 437 0742

Legends 1-10

London June 1976	English Chamber Orchestra	LP: DG 2530 786/2740 238 CD: DG 423 9191

Legend No 10

London   Philharmonia   78: HMV C 7822/DB 4317/DB 4328
May 1950

My Home, Overture

Munich   Bavarian RO   LP: DG 2530 593/2740 238
December 1973-   CD: DG 435 0742
June 1974

The Noon Day Witch

Munich   Bavarian RO   LP: DG 2530 712/2740 238
June 1974   CD: DG 435 0742

Othello, Overture

Prague   Czech PO   78: HMV JOX 7-8
October 1946

Munich   Bavarian RO   LP: DG 2530 785/2740 238
February 1976   CD: DG 435 0742

Scherzo capriccioso

London   Philharmonia   78: HMV C 7822-7823/DB 4316-4317
August-
September 1949

London   RPO   LP: HMV ALP 1769/ASD 347
November 1958   LP: Electrola E 70393/STE 70393

Munich   Bavarian RO   LP: DG 2530 466/2740 238
December 1973   CD: DG 423 1202/427 2022

Slavonic Dances op 46

Vienna   VPO   LP: Decca LXT 5079-5080
March 1955   Excerpts
                                      45: Decca 45-71115/CEP 534

Munich   Bavarian RO   LP: DG 2530 466/2740 238
December 1973   Excerpts
                                      LP: DG 2535 632
                                      CD: DG 427 2162/439 4362

Slavonic Dances op 72

Vienna   VPO   LP: Decca LXT 5079-5080
March 1955   Excerpts
                                    45: Decca CEP 534

Munich   Bavarian RO   LP: DG 2530 593/2740 238/2535 632
December 1973-   CD: DG 419 0562
June 1974   Excerpts
                                    CD: DG 439 4362

Slavonic Rhapsody No 3

London   RPO   LP: HMV ALP 1769/ASD 437
November 1958   LP: Electrola E 70393/STE 70393

The Water Goblin

Munich   Bavarian RO   LP: DG 2530 712/2740 238
June 1974   CD: DG 435 0742

The Wood Dove

Munich   Bavarian RO   LP: DG 2530 713/2740 238
June 1974   CD: DG 423 1202/435 0742/439 6632

MANUEL DE FALLA (1876-1946)

Noches en los jardines de Espana

Munich	Bavarian RO	LP: DG LPEM 19 116/SLPEM 139 116
June 1965	Weber	LP: DG 135 116/135 134/2535 268

JOSEF FOERSTER (1859-1951)

Symphony No 4

Prague	Czech PO	78: Supraphon/Ultraphon
1946		CD: Supraphon awaiting publication

CHRISTOPH WILLIBALD GLUCK (1714-1787)

Iphigenia in Aulis, Overture

London	Philharmonia	78: HMV DB 9753-9754
February 1952		

Iphigenia auf Tauris

Munich	Bavarian Radio	CD: Myto MCD 91544
March 1965	Orchestra & Chorus	Excerpts
	Jurinac, Fahberg,	LP: DG 2700 709
	Wunderlich, Prey,	CD: DG 435 1452
	Engen	

EDVARD GRIEG (1843-1907)

Piano Concerto

Berlin	BPO	LP: DG LPM 18 888/SLPM 138 888/2726 021
September 1963	Anda	CD: DG 413 1582/415 8502/439 4272

GEORGE FRIDERIC HANDEL (1685-1759)

Judas Maccabaeus

Munich October 1963	Bavarian Radio Orchestra & Chorus Giebel, Falk, Wunderlich, Pöld, Welter Sung in German	LP: Movimento musica 02.025 CD: Melodram MEL 28026

Serse

Munich October 1962	Bavarian Radio Orchestra & Chorus Hallstein, Cook, Töpper, Wunderlich, Kohn, Pröbstl Sung in German	CD: Verona 27032-27034 Excerpts LP: DG 2700 709 CD: DG 435 1452 CD: Melodram MEL 28026

Music for the Royal Fireworks

Berlin March 1963	BPO	LP: DG LPM 18 864/SLPM 138 864 LP: DG 2535 286/2726 520/413 9861 CD: DG 419 8612 Excerpts LP: DG 135 136/2535 642/2721 180

Water Music

Berlin March 1963	BPO	LP: DG LPM 18 799/SLPM 138 799/109 105 LP: DG 9103/2535 137/2726 520/413 9861 CD: DG 419 8612 Excerpts LP: DG LPM 18 864/SLPM 138 864 LP: DG 2535 642/2721 180

KARL AMADEUS HARTMANN (1905-1963)

Symphony No 4

Munich June 1967	Bavarian RO	LP: DG 139 359

Symphony No 8

Munich June 1967	Bavarian RO	LP: DG 139 359

Gesangsszene für Bariton und Orchester

Munich 1968	Bavarian RO Fischer-Dieskau	LP: Wergo WER 60061 CD: Wergo WER 60187-50

JOSEF HAYDN (1732-1809)

Symphony No 99

Munich May 1982	Bavarian RO	CD: Orfeo C206 891B

Cello Concerto in D, arranged by Gevaert

London May 1951	Philharmonia Fournier	78: HMV DB 21448-50/DB 9743-45 auto 45: Victor WHMV 1043 LP: Victor LHMV 1043

Trumpet Concerto in E flat

London September 1951	Philharmonia Jackson	HMV unpublished

Mass No 3 "Saint Cecilia"

Ottobeuren July 1982	Bavarian Radio Orchestra & Chorus Popp, Soffel, Laubenthal, Moll	Unpublished video recording <u>Rehearsals in Munich also filmed and used</u> <u>in a TV documentary about the conductor</u> <u>(see Miscellaneous section at the end of</u> <u>this discography</u>)

Mass No 7 "Missa in tempore belli"

Munich May 1963	Bavarian Radio Orchestra & Chorus Morison, M.Thomas, Witsch, Kohn	LP: DG LPM 18 881/SLPM 138 881/2535 442 <u>Excerpts</u> LP: DG 136 491/2535 609/2535 632

Die Schöpfung

Munich June 1984	Bavarian Radio Orchestra & Chorus Marshall, Popp, Cole, Weikl, Howell	CD: Orfeo C150 852H

PAUL HINDEMITH (1895-1963)

Mathis der Maler

Munich June and December 1977	Bavarian Radio Orchestra & Chorus Koszut, Wagemann, T.Schmidt, King, M.Schmidt, Cochran, Grobe, Feldhoff, Fischer-Dieskau, Malta	LP: EMI SLS 5182/1C 165 03515-03517 CD: EMI CDS 555 2372 Excerpt CD: EMI CMS 565 6212

Mathis der Maler, symphony

Date not confirmed	Bavarian RO	CD: Originals SH 804

Symphonic Metamorphoses on themes by Weber

Chicago April 1953	Chicago SO	LP: Mercury MG 50024/SR 176114 LP: HMV ALP 1251

Der Schwanendreher, for viola and orchestra

Date not confirmed	Bavarian RO Schmid	CD: Originals SH 804

ROYAL ALBERT HALL
Manager - C. S. Taylor

PHILHARMONIA CONCERT SOCIETY
President:
H.H. THE MAHARAJA OF MYSORE

Thursday, April 24, at 7.30 p.m.

FURTWÄNGLER
FLAGSTAD

SCHUMANN: Manfred Overture
SCHUMANN: Symphony No. 4
RAVEL: Rhapsodie Espagnol

WAGNER: Five Wesendonck Songs
WAGNER: Closing Scene from Götterdämmerung

Tuesday, June 3, at 7.30 p.m.

KUBELIK
SOLOMON

DVORAK: Scherzo Capriccioso
BRAHMS: Concerto in B flat, No. 2

DVORAK: Symphony No. 5 in E minor — New World

PHILHARMONIA
ORCHESTRA
Founder and Artistic Director: WALTER LEGGE

TICKETS: 12/6, 10/6, 7/6, 6/-, 3/6 and 2/6
From ROYAL ALBERT HALL (KEN. 8212); Chappell's Box Office, 50 New Bond Street, W.1, usual Ticket Offices, and
IBBS & TILLETT LTD., 124 Wigmore Street, W.1 (WELbeck 8418)

BAYERISCHE STAATSOPER
NATIONALTHEATER MÜNCHEN

MÜNCHNER FESTSPIELE 1970

Dienstag, 14. Juli 1970

Neuinszenierung

Die Zauberflöte

Oper in zwei Aufzügen von Emanuel Schikaneder

Musik von

WOLFGANG AMADEUS MOZART

Musikalische Leitung: Rafael Kubelik   Inszenierung: Günther Rennert

Bühnenbild: Josef Svoboda · Kostüme: Erich Kondrak   Tiermasken: Annelies Corrodi

Chöre: Wolfgang Baumgart

LEOS JANACEK (1854-1928)

Jenufa

Munich March 1970	Bavarian State Orchestra & Chorus Hillebrecht, Varnay, Benningsen, Cox, Cochran Sung in German	CD: Myto MCD 90422

Jenufa, extracts

London February 1968	Covent Garden Orchestra Collier, Varnay, Bainbridge, Cassilly, Lanigan Sung in English	CD: Myto MCD 90422

Glagolithic Mass

Munich November 1964	Bavarian Radio Orchestra & Chorus Lear, Rössl-Majdan, Haefliger, Crass	LP: DG LPM 18 954/SLPM 138 954 CD: DG 429 1822

Glagolithic Mass, Credo and Sanctus

Lucerne August 1960	Lucerne Festival Orchestra & Chorus Schech, Conrad, Haefliger, Robinson	CD: Relief CR 1881

Diary of a man who disappeared

Munich November 1963	Griffel, Haefliger Kubelik, piano	LP: DG LPM 18 904/SLPM 138 904/2543 820

Sinfonietta

Prague October 1946	Czech PO	78: HMV C 3573-3575/C 7671-7673 auto
Vienna March 1955	VPO	LP: Decca LW 5213
Munich May 1970	Bavarian RO	LP: DG 2530 075/410 9931 CD: DG 437 2542

Taras Bulba

London April 1958	RPO	LP: HMV ALP 1675 CD: EMI CZS 568 2232
Munich May 1970	Bavarian RO	LP: DG 2530 075 CD: DG 429 1822

Capriccio for piano and wind instruments

Munich 1971	Members of Bavarian RO Firkusny	LP: DG 2721 251

Concerto for piano and chamber ensemble

Munich 1971	Members of Bavarian RO Firkusny	LP: DG 2721 251

VOJTECH JIROVEK (1763-1850)

Symphony in E flat

Prague 1946	Czech PO	78: Supraphon/Ultraphon MBA 13038-13040

ARAM KHACHATURIAN (1903-1978)

Violin Concerto

Prague 1947	Prague RO D.Oistrakh	CD: Multisonic 31 00382 CD: Praga PR 25 0017

RAFAEL KUBELIK (born 1914)

Cantata without words

Munich May 1981	Bavarian Radio Orchestra & Chorus	CD: Panton 81 12642

4 forme per archi

London May 1969	English Chamber Orchestra	LP: DG 139 443

Inventions and Interludes, for childrens' chorus and wind instruments

Prague October- November 1993	Instrumentalists Kühn Childrens' Choir	CD: Panton 81 12642

Orphikon, symphony in 3 movements

Munich May-June 1984	Bavarian RO	CD: Panton 81 12642

FRANZ LISZT (1811-1886)

Piano Concerto No 1

Turin April 1961	RAI Torino Orchestra Michelangeli	LP: Movimento musica 01.004 CD: Frequenz 041.009 CD: Cetra CDAR 2003

Totentanz for piano and orchestra

Turin April 1961	RAI Torino Orchestra Michelangeli	LP: Movimento musica 01.004

GUSTAV MAHLER (1860-1911)

Symphony No 1

Vienna June 1954	VPO	LP: Decca LXT 2973/ACL 188/ECS 503
Munich October 1967	Bavarian RO	LP: DG 139 331/2720 063/2535 172 CD: DG 429 0422/429 1572/439 4102
Munich 1975	Bavarian RO	CD: Originals SH 843
London April 1976	LSO	Unpublished radio broadcast

Symphony No 2 "Resurrection"

Munich February 1969	Bavarian Radio Orchestra & Chorus Mathis, Procter	LP: DG 2720/2726 062 CD: DG 429 0422/445 0172

Symphony No 3

Munich May 1967	Bavarian Radio Orchestra & Chorus M.Thomas	LP: DG 139 337-139 338/2720 063/2726 063 CD: DG 429 0422

Symphony No 4

Munich April 1968	Bavarian RO Morison	LP: DG 139 339/2720 063/2535 119 CD: DG 429 0422/431 1652

Symphony No 5

Munich January 1971	Bavarian RO	LP: DG 2707 056/2720 063/2726 064/2543 535 CD: DG 429 0422/429 5912 <u>Adagietto</u> LP: DG 2535 624

Symphony No 6

Munich December 1968	Bavarian RO	LP: DG 2707 037/2720 063/2726 065 CD: DG 429 0422 /445 0382

Symphony No 7

Munich November 1970	Bavarian RO	LP: DG 22707 061/2720 063/2726 066 CD: DG 429 0422

Symphony No 8 "Symphony of a Thousand"

Munich June 1970	Bavarian Radio Orchestra & Chorus NDR & WDR Choruses Arroyo, Spoorenberg, Mathis, Hamari, Procter, Grobe, Crass, Fischer-Dieskau	LP: DG 2720 063/2726 053 CD: DG 419 4332/429 0422/447 5292

Symphony No 9

Munich March 1967	Bavarian RO	LP: DG 139 345-139 346/2707 038 LP: DG 2720 063/2726 067 CD: DG 429 0422 /445 0182
Date not confirmed	Bavarian RO	CD: Originals SH 806-807

Symphony No 10, Adagio

Munich	Bavarian RO	LP: DG 2707 037/2720 063/2726 053
March 1967		CD: DG 429 0422

Das Lied von der Erde

Date not	Bavarian RO	CD: Originals SH 806-807
confirmed	Baker, Kmennt	

Lieder eines fahrenden Gesellen

Munich	Bavarian RO	LP: DG 2707 056/2720 063/2530 630/2726 064
December 1968	Fischer-Dieskau	CD: DG 415 1912/439 4102

GIAN FRANCESCO MALIPIERO (1882-1973)

Concerto for 2 pianos and orchestra

Paris	Orchestre National	CD: Olympia OCD 270
1957	Reding, Piette	

JEAN MARTINON (1910-1976)

Violin Concerto

Munich	Bavarian RO	LP: DG 2530 033
December 1969	Szeryng	

BOHUSLAV MARTINU (1890-1959)

Symphony No 4 (1945)

Prague	Czech PO	78: Supraphon H 22951-22954/2050-2053
1946		78: Ultraphon G 15150-15153
		CD: Supraphon awaiting publication

Concerto for double string orchestra, piano and timpani

London	Philharmonia	78: HMV C 7911-7913
May 1950		

Fantasie concertante for piano and orchestra

Munich	Bavarian RO	LP: DG LPM 19 116/SLPM 139 116
June 1965	M.Weber	

Les fresques de Piero della Francesca

London	RPO	LP: HMV ALP 1675
April 1958		CD: EMI CZS 568 2232

FELIX MENDELSSOHN-BARTHOLDY (1809-1847)

Piano Concerto No 1

London October 1948	Philharmonia Lympany	78: HMV C 3838-3839 45: Victor WHMV 1025 LP: Victor LHMV 1025 LP: EMI HLM 7179 CD: EMI CDCFP 4650

Meeresstille glückliche Fahrt, Overture

London August 1949	Philharmonia	78: HMV C 7836-7837

Die schöne Melusine, Overture

London September 1952	Philharmonia	HMV unpublished

A Midsummer Night's Dream, incidental music

Munich November 1964	Bavarian Radio Orchestra & Chorus Mathis, Boese	LP: DG LPM 18 959/SLPM 138 959/2535 393 CD: DG 415 8402 <u>Excerpts</u> LP: DG 135 003/135 015/135 017 LP: DG 2535 634/2535 637/2721 073

A Midsummer Night's Dream, Overture, Nocturne and Wedding March

London September 1951- February 1952	Philharmonia	LP: HMV ALP 1049

A Midsummer Night's Dream, Scherzo

London May 1950	Philharmonia	78: HMV C 7836 LP: HMV ALP 1049

WOLFGANG AMADEUS MOZART (1756-1791)

Symphony No 25

Würzburg June 1981	Bavarian RO	CD: Orfeo C206 891B/C286 921Z

Symphony No 34

Chicago December 1952	Chicago SO	LP: Mercury MG 50015 LP: HMV ALP 1239 LP: Mercury Wing MGW 14022/SRW 18022 LP: Philips Wing WL 1015 LP: Philips SFL 14052

Symphony No 35 "Haffner"

Vienna January 1961	VPO	LP: HMV ALP 2069/ALP 617 CD: EMI CDZ 767 0092/CES 568 5312 CD: Royal Classics ROY 6410
Munich June 1980	Bavarian RO	LP: CBS 79331 CD: Sony MDK 44647

Symphony No 36 "Linz"

Vienna January 1961	VPO	LP: HMV ALP 1882/ASD 451 CD: EMI CDZ 767 0092/CES 568 5312 CD: Royal Classics ROY 6410
Munich October 1980	Bavarian RO	LP: CBS 79331 CD: Sony MDK 44647

Symphony No 38 "Prague"

Chicago April 1953	Chicago SO	LP: Mercury MG 50015 LP: HMV ALP 1239 LP: Mercury Wing MGW 14022/SRW 18022 LP: Philips Wing WL 1015 LP: Philips SFL 14052
Vienna January 1961	VPO	LP: HMV ALP 1882/ASD 451 CD: EMI CDZ 767 0102/CES 568 5312
Munich October 1980	Bavarian RO	LP: CBS 79331 CD: Sony MDK 44648
Munich May 1985	Bavarian RO	CD: Orfeo C206 891B
Prague 1991	Czech PO	CD: Denon CO-79728

Symphony No 39

Munich June 1980	Bavarian RO	LP: CBS 79331 CD: Sony MDK 44648

Symphony No 40

Munich October 1980	Bavarian RO	LP: CBS 79331 CD: Sony MDK 44649

Symphony No 41 "Jupiter"

Vienna January 1961	VPO	LP: HMV ALP 2069/ASD 617 CD: EMI CDZ 767 0102/CES 568 5312
Date not confirmed	Bavarian RO	CD: Originals SH 800
Munich June 1980	Bavarian RO	LP: CBS 79331 CD: Sony MDK 44649

Clarinet Concerto

Berlin   BPO   LP: DG 136 550/2535 188
October 1967   Leister   CD: DG 445 0222

Piano Concerto No 20

Munich   Bavarian RO   CD: Live Classic Best (Japan) LBC 137
1981   Perahia

Piano Concerto No 21

Würzburg   Bavarian RO   CD: Hunt CDMP 4941
June 1971   Casadesus

Piano Concerto No 23

Munich   Bavarian RO   CD: Live Classic Best (Japan) LBC 137
1976   Perahia

Violin Concerto No 3

London   RPO   LP: HMV ALP 1856/ASD 429
January and   de Vito
November 1959

Serenade No 7 "Haffner"

Munich   Bavarian RO   LP: DG LPM 18 869/SLPM 138 869/2535 139
April 1963

Serenade No 13 "Eine kleine Nachtmusik"

Vienna   VPO   LP: HMV ALP 1963/ASD 514
November 1960   CD: EMI CDZ 767 0092/CES 568 5312
                                   CD: Royal Classics ROY 6410

Andante (Cassation K63)

Vienna	VPO	LP: HMV ALP 1963/ASD 514
January 1961		CD: EMI CDZ 767 0102/CES 568 5312

La Clemenza di Tito, Overture

London	Philharmonia	78: HMV DB 21556
September 1952		45: HMV 7R 156
		LP: HMV ALP 1109

Cosi fan tutte, Overture

London	Philharmonia	78: HMV DB 21556
September 1952		45: HMV 7R 156
		LP: HMV ALP 1109

Don Giovanni

Munich	Bavarian Radio	LP: Eurodisc 302 435-445
May 1985	Orchestra & Chorus	CD: Eurodisc 353 263/610 287 233
	Varady, Auger,	CD: RCA/BMG RG 77982/74321 252842
	Mathis, T.Moser,	
	Titus, Panerai	

Don Giovanni, Overture

London	Philharmonia	LP: HMV ALP 1109
September 1952		

Die Entführung aus dem Serail, Overture

London	Philharmonia	78: HMV DB 9753
February 1952		LP: HMV ALP 1109

La finta giardiniera, Overture

London	Philharmonia	LP: HMV ALP 1109
September 1952		

Idomeneo, Overture

London	Philharmonia	78: HMV DB 21465
May 1951		45: HMV 7ER 5002
		LP: HMV ALP 1109

Le Nozze di Figaro, Overture

London	Philharmonia	78: HMV DB 21548
September 1952		LP: HMV ALP 1109

Der Schauspieldirektor, Overture

London	Philharmonia	78: HMV DB 21548
September 1952		LP: HMV ALP 1109

Die Zauberflöte, Overture

London	Philharmonia	45: HMV 7ER 5002
September 1952		LP: HMV ALP 1109

Ave verum corpus

Munich	Bavarian RO	LP: DG 2530 356/2535 654/2545 055
September 1968	Regensburg Choir	LP: DG 2563 632/2721 073

Mass No 10 "Spatzenmesse"

Munich	Bavarian RO	LP: DG 2530 356
September 1968	Regensburg Choir	CD: DG 419 0602
	Mathis, Troyanos,	
	Laubenthal, Engen	

Mass No 16 "Coronation"

Munich	Bavarian Radio	LP: DG 2530 356
February 1973	Orchestra & Chorus	CD: DG 419 0602
	Mathis, Proctor,	
	Grobe, Shirley-Quirk	

MODEST MUSSORGSKY (1839-1881)

Pictures at an Exhibition

Chicago April 1951	Chicago SO	LP: Mercury MG 50000/SR 176114 LP: HMV BLP 1002
Munich 1970	Bavarian RO	CD: Originals SH 848

Boris Godunov

London November 1958	Covent Garden Orchestra & Chorus Resnik, Gostic, Lanigan, Christoff, Rouleau, Kelly	Unpublished radio broadcast

OTTO NICOLAI (1810-1849)

Die lustigen Weiber von Windsor

Munich April 1977	Bavarian Radio Orchestra & Chorus Donath, T.Schmidt, Ahnsjö, Zednik, Ridderbusch, Brendel, Malta	LP: Decca D86 D3 CD: Decca 443 6692 Excerpts CD: Decca 444 8832 Recording also used as soundtrack to a filmed version of the opera

CARL NIELSEN (1865-1931)

Symphony No 5

Copenhagen June 1983	Danish RO	LP: EMI EL 27 03521 CD: EMI CDM 565 1822

CARL ORFF (1895-1982)

Oedipus der Tyrann

Munich 1966	Bavarian Radio Orchestra & Chorus Varnay, Stolze, Harper, Engen, Kohn, Nöcker	LP: DG 139 251-139 253/2709 025/2740 227

HANS PFITZNER (1869-1949)

Palestrina

Munich January-February 1973	Bavarian Radio Orchestra & Chorus Donath, Fassbaender, Gedda, Weikl, Fischer-Dieskau, Ridderbusch, Prey	LP: DG 2711 013/2740 223 CD: DG 427 4172

SERGEI PROKOFIEV (1891-1953)

Violin Concerto No 1

Prague 1947	Prague SO D.Oistrakh	CD: Multisonic 31 00382

ARNOLD SCHOENBERG (1874-1951)

Gurrelieder

Munich March 1965	Bavarian Radio Orchestra & Chorus Borkh, Töpper, Schachtschneider, Fehenberger, Engen, Fiedler	LP: DG 2707 022/2726 046 CD: DG 431 7442

5 pieces for orchestra

Chicago April 1953	Chicago SO	LP: Mercury MG 50024 LP: HMV ALP 1251

Piano Concerto

Munich	Bavarian RO	LP: DG 2530 257/2543 801
December 1971	Brendel	CD: DG 431 7402

Violin Concerto

Munich	Bavarian RO	LP: DG 2530 257/2543 801
September 1971	Zeitlin	CD: DG 431 7402

FRANZ SCHUBERT (1797-1828)

Symphony No 3

Vienna	VPO	LP: HMV ALP 1844
January 1960		LP: Electrola E 91154/STE 91154

Symphony No 4 "Tragic"

Vienna	VPO	LP: HMV ALP 1844
January 1960		LP: Electrola E 91154/STE 91154
		CD: EMI CES 568 5342

Symphony No 8 "Unfinished"

Vienna	VPO	LP: HMV ALP 1963/ASD 514
November 1960		LP: Electrola E 70439/STE 70439
		LP: EMI 1C 053 00651
		CD: EMI CES 568 5342

Symphony No 9 "Great"

London	RPO	LP: HMV ALP 1751/ASD 325
November 1958		LP: Electrola E 91054/STE 91054
		<u>Third movement</u>
		LP: HMV CLP 1840
Date not confirmed	Bavarian RO	CD: Artists' Live Recordings FED 065

ROBERT SCHUMANN (1810-1856)

Symphony No 1 "Spring"

Berlin February 1963	BPO	LP: DG LPM 18 860/SLPM 138 860 LP: DG 2709 034/2535 116 CD: DG 437 3952
Munich May 1979	Bavarian RO	LP: CBS 79323 CD: Sony MYK 42603/M2YK 45680/SBK 48269

Symphony No 2

Berlin September 1964	BPO	LP: DG LPM 18 955/SLPM 138 955 LP: DG 2709 034/2535 117 CD: DG 429 5202/437 3952
Munich May 1979	Bavarian RO	LP: CBS 79323 CD: Sony M2YK 45680/SBK 48269

Symphony No 3 "Rhenish"

Berlin February 1964	BPO	LP: DG LPM 18 908/SLPM 138 908 LP: DG 2709 034/2535 118 LP: Contour CC 7538 CD: DG 429 5202/437 3952
Munich May 1979	Bavarian RO	LP: CBS 79323 CD: Sony MYK 42603/M2YK 45680/SBK 48270

Symphony No 4

Berlin February 1963	BPO	LP: DG LPM 18 860/SLPM 138 860 LP: DG 2709 034/2535 116 CD: DG 437 3952/445 0192
Munich September 1978	Bavarian RO	LP: CBS 79323 CD: Sony M2YK 45680/SBK 48270

Piano Concerto

Berlin September 1963	BPO Anda	LP: DG LPM 18 888/SLPM 138 888 CD: DG 415 8502
Munich 1975	Bavarian RO Kempff	LP: DG 2530 484

Introduction and Allegro appassionato for piano and orchestra

Munich 1975	Bavarian RO Kempff	LP: DG 2530 484

Genoveva, Overture

Berlin September 1964	BPO	LP: DG LPM 18 955/SLPM 138 955 LP: DG 2709 034/2535 117

Manfred, Overture

Berlin February 1964	BPO	LP: DG LPM 18 908/SLPM 138 908 LP: DG 2709 034/135 003/2535 118 LP: Contour CC 7538 CD: DG 437 3952

NATIONAL ORCHESTRA OF CZECHOSLOVAKIA

PRAGUE PHILHARMONIC ORCHESTRA

CONDUCTED BY

RAFAEL KUBELIK

TWO LONDON CONCERTS
QUEEN'S HALL, Nov. 10 & 15

THIS FAMOUS ORCHESTRA WILL ALSO APPEAR IN THE FOLLOWING TOWNS
in the
INTERNATIONAL CELEBRITY SUBSCRIPTION CONCERTS

BIRMINGHAM	NOV. 2
GLASGOW	NOV. 3
ABERDEEN	NOV. 4
EDINBURGH	NOV. 5
MANCHESTER	NOV. 6
MIDDLESBRO	NOV. 7
NEWCASTLE	NOV. 8
SHEFFIELD	NOV. 9
DUBLIN	NOV. 12
LIVERPOOL	NOV. 13
HANLEY	NOV. 14
NOTTINGHAM	NOV. 16
SOUTHAMPTON	NOV. 17
BRISTOL	NOV. 19
CARDIFF	NOV. 20

1938 concerts

QUEEN'S HALL
Sole Lessees - Messrs. Chappell & Co. Ltd.

HAROLD HOLT presents the

NATIONAL ORCHESTRA OF CZECHOSLOVAKIA

PRAGUE PHILHARMONIC ORCHESTRA

Thursday, NOVEMBER 10 at 8.30

Programme

Overture—"Carnaval Romain"	H. BERLOIZ
Symphony in D minor	C. FRANCK
Symphonic Poem—"Sarka"	B. SMETANA
Serenade for Strings	A. DVORAK
Slavonic Dances	A. DVORAK

Tuesday, NOVEMBER 15 at 8.30

Programme

Overture—"Prodana nevesta" (The Bartered Bride) B. SMETANA
Symphony No. 2 in D minor "Pathetique" ...A. DVORAK
Pianoforte Concerto No. 2 ... B. MARTINU
FIRKUSNY
Suite Slovaque ... ... V. NOVAK
Snow Maiden "Dance of the Tumblers" RIMSKY KORSAKOV

Conductor
RAFAEL KUBELIK

BEDRICH SMETANA (1824-1884)

Ma Vlast

Chicago December 1952	Chicago SO	LP: Mercury MRL 2504-2505 Excerpts LP: Mercury Wing MGW 14026/MGW 14037 LP: Mercury Wing SRW 18026/SRW 18037 LP: Philips Wing WL 1018 CD: RCA/BMG GD 60206
Vienna April 1958	VPO	LP: Decca LXT 5474-5475/SXL 2064-2065 LP: Decca ADD 161-162/SDD 161-162 CD: Belart 450 0602 Excerpts 45: Decca CEP 568 LP: Decca BR 3104/SWL 8014/ECS 771
Rome 1970	RAI Roma Orchestra	CD: Live Classic Best (Japan) LCB 107
Boston March 1971	Boston SO	LP: DG 2707 054/2726 515 CD: DG 429 1832 Excerpts LP: DG 2535 132/2535 632/2538 313/2721 216 CD: DG 427 2162/439 4512/439 6632
Munich May 1984	Bavarian RO	CD: Orfeo C115 842H
Prague May 1990	Czech PO	CD: Supraphon 11 1208-2031/11 1895-2034

Ma Vlast, From Bohemia's Woods and Fields & The Moldau

Prague 1937	Czech PO	78: HMV C 2979-2981 78: Victor M 523

Ma Vlast: Vysherad, Sarka, Tabor and Blanik

London November 1947	BBCSO	Unpublished radio broadcast

The Bartered Bride, Overture

London September 1951	Philharmonia	78: HMV DB 21463 45: HMV 7ER 5015/7P 224 LP: HMV ALP 1049
London February 1952	Philharmonia	HMV unpublished

The Bartered Bride, Dance of the Comedians

London September 1951- February 1952	Philharmonia	78: HMV DB 21464 45: HMV 7ER 5010 LP: HMV ALP 1049

The Bartered Bride, Polka

London September 1951	Philharmonia	45: HMV 7ER 5010 LP: HMV ALP 1049

The Bartered Bride, Furiant

London September 1951	Philharmonia	78: HMV DB 21463 45: HMV 7ER 5010/7P 224 LP: HMV ALP 1049

Carnival in Prague

Munich December 1971	Bavarian RO	LP: DG 2530 248/2543 814 CD: DG 437 2542

Haakon Jarl

Prague 1946	Czech PO	78: Supraphon/Ultraphon G 14054-14055 78: Supraphon/Ultraphon G 22153-22154 78: Elite 9006-9007 CD: Supraphon awaiting publication
Munich December 1971	Bavarian RO	LP: DG 2530 248/2543 814 CD: DG 437 2542

Richard III

Prague 1946	Czech PO	78: Supraphon/Ultraphon G 14050-14051 78: Supraphon/Ultraphon G 22149-22150 78: Elite 9004-9005 CD: Supraphon awaiting publication
Munich December 1971	Bavarian RO	LP: DG 2530 248/2543 814 CD: DG 437 2542

Wallenstein's Camp

Prague 1946	Czech PO	78: Supraphon/Ultraphon G 14052-14053 78: Supraphon/Ultraphon G 22151-22152 78: Elite 9001-9002 78: Mercury DM 11 LP: Mercury MG 10013 LP: Symphonic (USA) SR 1 CD: Supraphon awaiting publication
Munich December 1971	Bavarian RO	LP: DG 2530 248/2543 814 CD: DG 437 2542

JOSEF SUK (1874-1935)

Mediation on the Chorale "Saint Wenceslas"

Prague 1946	Czech PO	78: Supraphon/Ultraphon CD: Supraphon awaiting publication

Legend of Dead Victors

Prague 1946	Czech PO	78: Supraphon/Ultraphon CD: Supraphon awaiting publication

Towards a New Life

Prague 1946	Czech PO	78: Supraphon/Ultraphon CD: Supraphon awaiting publication

PIOTR TCHAIKOVSKY (1840-1893)

Symphony No 4

Chicago November 1951	Chicago SO	LP: Mercury MG 50003 LP: HMV ALP 1083 LP: Mercury Wing MGW 14024/SRW 18024
Vienna January 1960	VPO	LP: HMV ALP 1815/ASD 398 LP: Electrola E 91132/STE 91132 CD: EMI CZS 252 2882/CZS 568 2232

Symphony No 5

Vienna November 1960	VPO	LP: HMV ALP 1859/ASD 428 LP: Electrola E 91135/STE 91135

Symphony No 6 "Pathétique"

Chicago April 1952	Chicago SO	LP: Mercury MG 50006/MRL 2000 LP: Mercury Wing MGW 14020/SRW 18020 LP: Philips Wing WL 1014
Vienna November 1960	VPO	LP: HMV ALP 1895/ASD 462 LP: Electrola E 91138/STE 91138 LP: EMI 5C 051 00960/1C 047 50518

Romeo and Juliet

Vienna March 1955	VPO	LP: Decca LXT 5079

ALEXANDER TCHEREPNIN (1899-1977)

Piano Concerto No 2

Munich March 1968	Bavarian RO Tcherepnin	LP: DG 139 379

Piano Concerto No 5

Munich March 1968	Bavarian RO Tcherepnin	LP: DG 139 379

RICHARD WAGNER (1813-1883)

Der fliegende Holländer: Excerpt (Die Frist ist um)

Munich June 1977	Bavarian RO Fischer-Dieskau	LP: EMI ASD 3499/1C 063 02969

Götterdämmerung

New York March 1974	Metropolitan Opera Orchestra & Chorus Hunter, Rankin, Dunn, Brilioth, Dooley, Rundgren, Rintzler	Unpublished Met broadcast

Lohengrin

Munich April 1971	Bavarian Radio Orchestra & Chorus Janowitz, Jones, King, Stewart, Ridderbusch, Nienstedt	LP: DG 2713 005/2720 036/2740 141/419 0291 CD: DG (Japan) POCG 2874-2876 Excerpts LP: DG 2535 026 CD: DG 445 0502

Lohengrin, Prelude

Berlin February 1963	BPO	LP: DG LPEM 19 228/SLPEM 136 228/2535 212 CD: DG 445 0562

Die Meistersinger von Nürnberg

Munich October 1967	Bavarian Radio Orchestra & Chorus Janowitz, Fassbaender, Konya, Unger, Stewart, Crass, Engen, Hemsley	CD: Myto MCD 92569

Die Meistersinger von Nürnberg, Overture

Berlin	BPO	LP: DG LPEM 19 228/SLPEM 136 228
February 1963		LP: DG 135 087/2535 212
		CD: DG 445 0562

Parsifal: Excerpt (Ja, wehe! Wehe!)

Munich	Bavarian RO	LP: EMI ASD 3499/1C 063 02969/EX 29 04323
June 1977	Fischer-Dieskau	CD: EMI CMS 565 6212

Parsifal: Excerpt (Lass' ihn unenthüllt!)

Munich	Bavarian Radio	LP: EMI ASD 3499/1C 063 02969
June 1977	Orchestra & Chorus	CD: EMI CMS 565 6212
	Fischer-Dieskau	

Siegfried Idyll

Berlin	BPO	LP: DG LPEM 19 228/SLPEM 136 228
February 1963		LP: DG 2535 212/2727 015
Munich	Bavarian RO	LP: CBS 35914-35915
November 1979		CD: Sony SMK 66930

Tannhäuser, Overture

Date not confirmed	Bavarian RO	CD: Artists' Live Recordings FED 065

Tristan und Isolde, Prelude and Liebestod

Berlin	BPO	LP: DG LPEM 19 228/SLPEM 136 228
February 1963		LP: DG 135 087/2535 212

Die Walküre: Excerpt (Leb' wohl, du kühnes herrliches Kind!)

Munich	Bavarian RO	LP: EMI ASD 3499/1C 063 02969/EX 29 04323
June 1977	Fischer-Dieskau	CD: EMI CMS 565 2122

CARL MARIA VON WEBER (1786-1826)

Clarinet Concerto No 1

Berlin	BPO	LP: DG 136 550/2538 087
November 1967	Leister	CD: DG 445 0222

Abu Hassan, Overture

Munich	Bavarian RO	LP: DG LPEM 19 463/SLPEM 136 465
March 1964		LP: DG 135 113/2535 136

Euryanthe, Overture

Munich	Bavarian RO	LP: DG LPEM 19 463/SLPEM 136 463
March 1964		LP: DG 135 113/2535 136/2535 634

Der Freischütz

Munich	Bavarian Radio	LP: Decca D235 D3
November 1979	Orchestra & Chorus	CD: Decca 417 119/443 6722
	Behrens, Donath,	<u>Excerpts</u>
	Kollo, Moll, Meven,	CD: Decca 444 8822
	Brendel	

Der Freischütz, Overture

Munich	Bavarian RO	LP: DG LPEM 19 463/SLPEM 136 463/135 040
March 1964		LP: DG 2535 136/2535 393/2535 602/2721 181
		CD: DG 415 8402

Jubel, Overture

Munich	Bavarian RO	LP: DG LPEM 19 463/SLPEM 136 463
March 1964		LP: DG 135 112/2535 136

Oberon

Munich March and December 1970	Bavarian Radio Orchestra & Chorus Nilsson, Auger, Hamari, Schiml, Domingo, Grobe, Prey	LP: DG 2709 035/2726 052 CD: DG 419 0382

Oberon, Overture

Munich March 1964	Bavarian RO	LP: DG LPEM 19 463/SLPEM 136 463/135 015 LP: DG 135 040/2535 136/2535 393 CD: DG 415 8402

Preciosa, Overture

Munich March 1964	Bavarian RO	LP: DG LPEM 19 463/SLPEM 136 463/2535 136

MISCELLANEOUS

Rafael Kubelik: Eine Begegnung

Ottobeuren July 1982	Unpublished video recording TV documentary by Percy Adlon, including sections from rehearsal and performance of Haydn's Saint Cecilia Mass (see under Haydn in the discography). Co-production between Pelemele Films and Bavarian Radio

Wednesday 12 May

Overture, Carneval

Violoncello concerto in B minor

Symphony No. 2, in D minor

PIERRE FOURNIER
SIR MALCOLM SARGENT

Wednesday 19 May

Concert performance of
RUSALKA
A Lyrical Fairy-tale in Three Acts

GRÉ BROUWENSTIJN
LAELIA FINNEBERG
NOREEN BERRY
ROWLAND JONES
NORMAN LUMSDEN
ADRIENNE COLE   MARION LOWE
PAMELA BOWDEN   FRANCIS LORING
BBC CHORUS
RAFAEL KUBELIK

Wednesday 26 May

Slavonic Rhapsody No. 3, in A Flat

Overture, Othello

Te Deum

Aria, Where art thou, father?
(The Spectre's Bride)

Symphony No. 4, in G

ELISABETH SCHWARZKOPF
BRUCE BOYCE
BBC CHORUS
BBC CHORAL SOCIETY
SIR MALCOLM SARGENT

Wednesday 2 June

Symphonic Variations

Violin concerto in A minor

Symphony No. 5, in E minor
(From the New World)

ENDRÉ WOLF
SIR MALCOLM SARGENT

London concerts to mark the 50th anniversary of Dvorak's death

André Cluytens
1905-1967

Discography compiled
by John Hunt

CARL PHILIPP EMANUEL BACH (1714-1788)

Cello Concerto No 3

Paris	Conservatoire	78: Columbia LX 1419-1421/8819-8821 auto
1950	Orchestra	78: Columbia (France) LFX 930-932
	Navarra	

LUDWIG VAN BEETHOVEN (1770-1827)

Symphony No 1

Berlin	BPO	LP: Electrola E 80034-80035/E 80539/ STE 80539
December 1958		LP: EMI CFP 187
		CD: Toshiba TOCE 1561

Symphony No 2

Berlin	BPO	LP: EMI CFP 193
April 1959		CD: Toshiba TOCE 1564
		Also issued on LP by Electrola

Symphony No 3 "Eroica"

Berlin	BPO	LP: EMI CFP 40076
December 1958		CD: Toshiba TOCE 1561
		Also issued on LP by Electrola

Symphony No 4

Berlin	BPO	LP: EMI XLP 30098/SXLP 30098/CFP 40001
May 1959		CD: Toshiba TOCE 1563
		Also issued on LP by Electrola

BAYREUTHER FESTSPIELE · DIENSTAG, 6. AUGUST 1957
RICHARD WAGNER · DIE MEISTERSINGER VON NÜRNBERG

HANS SACHS	GUSTAV NEIDLINGER
EVA	ELISABETH GRÜMMER
WALTHER VON STOLZING	WALTER GEISLER
VEIT POGNER	GOTTLOB FRICK
SIXTUS BECKMESSER	KARL SCHMITT-WALTER
FRITZ KOTHNER	TONI BLANKENHEIM
DAVID	GERHARD STOLZE
MAGDALENA	GEORGINE V. MILINKOVIC
KUNZ VOGELGESANG	FRITZ UHL
BALTHASAR ZORN	HEINZ-GÜNTHER ZIMMERMANN
ULRICH EISSLINGER	ERICH BENKE
AUGUSTIN MOSER	HERMANN WINKLER
KONRAD NACHTIGALL	EGMONT KOCH
HERMANN ORTEL	HANS HABIETINEK
HANS SCHWARZ	ALEXANDER FENYVES
HANS FOLTZ	EUGEN FUCHS
EIN NACHTWÄCHTER	ARNOLD VAN MILL
AUF DER FESTWIESE	HARALD KREUTZBERG UND DIE TANZGRUPPEN
MUSIKALISCHE LEITUNG	ANDRÉ CLUYTENS
REGIE UND INSZENIERUNG	WIELAND WAGNER
CHOREINSTUDIERUNG	WILHELM PITZ
REGIE-ASSISTENZ UND CHOREOGRAPHIE	GERTRUD WAGNER
MUSIKALISCHE ASSISTENZ	MAXIMILIAN KOJETINSKY · ROLF REINHARDT
KOSTÜM	KURT PALM
TECHNISCHE LEITUNG UND BELEUCHTUNG	PAUL EBERHARDT
MASKE	WILLI KLOSE
LEITER DES DEKORATIONSWESENS	JOHANNES DREHER
KASCHIERARBEITEN	GUSTAV JÄGER

DER BEGINN JEDES AUFZUGS WIRD 15 MINUTEN VORHER MIT EINER FANFARE, 10 MINUTEN VORHER MIT ZWEI UND 5 MINUTEN VORHER MIT DREI FANFAREN ANGEKÜNDIGT
BEGINN 16.00 UHR · 1. AUFZUG 18.30 UHR · 3. AUFZUG 20.40 UHR · ENDE GEGEN 22.40 UHR · NACH BEGINN DER AUFZÜGE KEIN EINLASS

Symphony No 5

Berlin December 1957- March 1958	BPO	LP: HMV ALP 1657/ASD 267 LP: Electrola E 80429/STE 80429 LP: EMI XLP 30081/SXLP 30081/CFP 40007 LP: EMI 1C 187 29281-29282 CD: Toshiba TOCE 1562

Symphony No 5, First movement

Vienna January- December 1958	VPO	45: HMV 7ER 5191/RES 4281 LP: HMV ALP 1736/ASD 304

Symphony No 6 "Pastoral"

Berlin March 1956	BPO	LP: HMV ALP 1408 LP: Electrola WALP 1515
Berlin March 1960	BPO	LP: HMV ALP 1863/ASD 433/CFP 40017 LP: Electrola E 80007/STE 80007 CD: EMI CZS 568 2212 CD: Toshiba TOCE 1563

Symphony No 7

Paris 1957	Conservatoire Orchestra	CD: Refrain (Japan) DR 92 0042
Berlin February 1957	BPO	LP: HMV ALP 1576/CFP 40018 LP: Electrola E 80019/STE 80019 CD: Toshiba TOCE 1564

Symphony No 8

Berlin December 1957- March 1958	BPO	LP: Electrola E 80539/STE 80539 LP: EMI XLP 30081/SXLP 30081/CFP 40007 CD: Toshiba TOCE 1562 <u>Also issued on a number of pirate labels,</u> <u>where it was described as a performance</u> <u>conducted by Wilhelm Furtwängler</u>

Symphony No 8, Second movement

Vienna January- December 1958	VPO	45: HMV 7ER 5195/RES 4284 LP: HMV ALP 1736/ASD 304

Symphony No 9 "Choral"

Berlin	BPO	LP: Electrola E 80034-80035
December 1957	St Hedwig's Choir	LP: EMI XLP 30085/SXLP 30085/CFP 40019
	Brouwenstijn,	LP: EMI 1C 053 11129/1C 063 11129
	Meyer, Gedda,	LP: Angel 60079
	Guthrie	CD: Toshiba TOCE 1565

Piano Concerto No 2

London	Philharmonia	LP: HMV BLP 1024/MFP 2067/SLS 5026
November 1952	Solomon	CD: EMI CDF 300 0402/CHS 565 5032
Berlin	BPO	CD: Myto MCD 89005
February 1956	Solomon	

Piano Concerto No 3

Paris	Conservatoire	LP: Columbia 33CX 1188
1953	Orchestra	LP: EMI 1C 153 11626-11627M
	Gilels	
Berlin	BPO	LP: EMI XLP 20045/SXLP 20045/CFP 135
January 1962	Tacchino	

Piano Concerto No 4

London	Philharmonia	LP: HMV BLP 1036/XLP 30020/SLS 5026
November 1952	Solomon	CD: EMI CDF 300 0042/CHS 565 5032
Paris	Orchestre National	LP: Discocorp RR 232
December 1955	Haskil	CD: Disques Montaigne TCE 8780
		CD: Seven Seas (Japan) KICC 2370
		CD: Music and Arts CD 863

Violin Concerto

Paris	Orchestre National	LP: Columbia 33CX 1672/SAX 2315
1959	D.Oistrakh	LP: Columbia (Germany) C 91051/STC 91051
		LP: EMI XLP 30168/SXLP 30168
		LP: EMI SHZE 143/SLS 5004
		CD: EMI CDM 769 2612

Coriolan, Overture

Berlin   BPO   LP: EMI CFP 187
April 1959   CD: EMI 252 5782

Egmont, Overture

Berlin   BPO   LP: HMV ALP 1576/CFP 193
February 1957   LP: Electrola E 80019/STE 80019

Fidelio, Overture

Berlin   BPO   LP: EMI XLP 30098/SXLP 30098/CFP 40001
November 1960

Die Geschöpfe des Prometheus, Overture

Paris   Conservatoire   78: Pathé PD 144/MD 3
1950   Orchestra   Probably also issued on LP by Pathé

Berlin   BPO   LP: EMI XLP 30098/SXLP 30098/CFP 40001
April 1959

Leonore No 3, Overture

Berlin   BPO   LP: HMV ALP 1657/ASD 267
May 1958   LP: Electrola E 80429/STE 80429
                                    LP: EMI XLP 30098/SXLP 30098/CFP 187
                                    CD: Toshiba TOCE 1562

Die Ruinen von Athen, Overture

Berlin   BPO   LP: EMI XLP 30098/SXLP 30098/CFP 40001
November 1960

HECTOR BERLIOZ (1803-1869)

Symphonie fantastique

Paris October 1955	Orchestre National	LP: Columbia 33CX 1439 CD: Musical Note (Japan) 18MN 1002
London November 1958	Philharmonia	LP: Columbia 33CX 1673 LP: EMI CFP 168 CD: EMI CDZ 762 6052

L'Enfance du Christ

Paris 1950-1951	Conservatoire Orchestra St Paul Choir Bouvier, Giraudeau, Roux	LP: Pathé DTX 101-102 LP: Vox PL 7120/PL 7122/VUX 2009
Paris November- December 1965 and September 1966	Conservatoire Orchestra Duclos Choir De los Angeles, Gedda, Blanc	LP: EMI AN 170-171/SAN 170-171 LP: Angel 3680 CD: EMI CZS 568 5862 Excerpts CD: EMI CZS 568 2212

La Damnation de Faust, extracts

Paris October 1959	Paris Opéra Orchestra & Chorus Gorr, Gedda, Souzay	LP: HMV ALP 1860/ASD 430/CFP 40039 LP: Angel 35941 LP: EMI 2C 061 11684 Marche hongroise CD: EMI 252 5782

La Damnation de Faust: Menuet des follets; Danse des sylphes; Marche hongroise

Paris September 1956	Paris Opéra Orchestra	LP: Columbia 33CX 1544 LP: EMI 2C 053 10771 CD: Toshiba CC30 3740-3741
Moscow May 1959	Orchestre National	LP: Melodiya M10 46303 002

Roméo et Juliette: Rêverie; Fête des Capulets; La reine Mab; Scène d'amour

Paris September 1956	Conservatoire Orchestra	LP: Columbia 33CX 1544 LP: EMI 2C 053 10771 <u>La reine Mab</u> CD: Toshiba CC33-3739

Béatrice et Bénédict, Overture

Paris 1956	Paris Opéra Orchestra	LP: Columbia 33CX 1524
Paris March 1961	Orchestre National	LP: Pathé CVD 3546 CD: Toshiba CC33-3739

Benvenuto Cellini, Overture

Paris 1956	Paris Opéra Orchestra	LP: Columbia 33CX 1524
Paris March 1961	Orchestre National	LP: Pathé CVD 3546 CD: Toshiba CC33-3739

Le carnaval romain, Overture

Paris 1956	Paris Opéra Orchestra	LP: Columbia 33CX 1524
Moscow May 1959	Orchestre National	LP: Melodiya M10 42679-42882
Paris March 1961	Orchestre National	LP: Pathé CVD 3546/2C 053 10771 CD: Toshiba CC33-3739 CD: EMI 252 5782

Le corsaire, Overture

Paris 1956	Paris Opéra Orchestra	LP: Columbia 33CX 1524
Paris March 1961	Orchestre National	LP: Pathé CVD 3546 CD: Toshiba CC33-3739

Le roi Lear, Overture

Paris 1956	Paris Opéra Orchestra	LP: Columbia 33CX 1524

Les Troyens, Chasse royale et orage

Paris September 1956	Conservatoire Orchestra Duclos Choir	LP: Pathé CVD 3546/2C 053 10771 CD: Toshiba CC33-3739

GEORGES BIZET (1838-1875)

Carmen

Paris October 1950	Opéra-Comique Orchestra & Chorus Michel, Angelici, Jobin, Dens	78: Columbia (USA) MOP 33 LP: Columbia (USA) SL 109 LP: Columbia 33CX 1016-1018 LP: Columbia (France) FCX 101-103 CD: EMI CMS 565 3182 <u>Excerpts</u> 45: Columbia SEL 1553/SEL 1558

Carmen, Suite

Paris January 1964	Conservatoire Orchestra	LP: Columbia 33CX 1925/SAX 2566 CD: Toshiba CC33-3401 <u>Act 1 Prelude</u> CD: EMI 252 5782

Les pêcheurs de perles

Paris June 1954	Opéra-Comique Orchestra & Chorus Angelici, Legay, Dens, Noguera	LP: Columbia 33CX 1232-1233 LP: Pathé 2C 153 12057-12058 CD: EMI CMS 565 2662

Symphony in C

Paris October 1953	Orchestre National	LP: Columbia 33CX 1173 CD: Musical Note (Japan) 18MN 1010
Moscow May 1959	Orchestre National	LP: Melodiya M10 42879-42882

L'Arlésienne, Suites Nos 1 and 2

Paris 1950-1951	Orchestre National	LP: Columbia 33CX 1153 CD: Musical Note (Japan) 18MN 1010 Excerpts 78: Pathé 45: Columbia SEL 1521
Paris January 1964	Conservatoire Orchestra	LP: Columbia 33CX 1925/SAX 2566 CD: Toshiba CC33-3401 Farandole CD: EMI 252 5782

Farandole (L'Arlésienne)

Moscow May 1959	Orchestre National	LP: Melodiya M10 46303 002

La jolie fille de Perth, Suite

Paris 1950-1951	Orchestre National	LP: Columbia 33CX 1153 CD: Musical Note (Japan) 18MN 1005

Patrie, Overture

Paris 1949	Conservatoire Orchestra	78: HMV (France) W 1609-1610
Paris October 1953	Orchestre National	LP: Columbia 33CX 1173 CD: Musical Note (Japan) 18MN 1005

EMMANUEL BONDEVILLE (born 1898)

Gaultier-Garguille, symphonic poem

Paris 1952-1953	Orchestre National	LP: Columbia (France) FCX 270

Madame Bovary, excerpts

Paris 1952-1953	Opéra-Comique Orchestra Brumaire, Dens, Rialland	LP: Columbia (France) FCX 270

ALEXANDER BORODIN (1833-1887)

In the Steppes of Central Asia

Paris 1949	Conservatoire Orchestra	78: Pathé PDT 280 LP: Pathé DTX 116 LP: Vox PL 7670
London November 1958	Philharmonia	LP: Columbia 33CX 1699/SAX 2355 LP: EMI XLP 20106/SXLP 20106 CD: EMI 252 5782/CDM 769 1102 CD: EMI CZS 568 5502

Polovtsian Dances (Prince Igor)

Paris September 1959	Conservatoire Orchestra	LP: Pathé CD: EMI CDM 769 1102

JOHANNES BRAHMS (1833-1897)

Piano Concerto No 2

Turin	RAI Torino	CD: Cetra ARCD 2037
May 1962	Orchestra	CD: Curcio-Hunt CON 14
	Rubinstein	Also issued on LP by Cetra

EMMANUEL CHABRIER (1841-1894)

Espana

London	Philharmonia	HMV unpublished
November 1952		

FREDERIC CHOPIN (1810-1849)

Andante spianato et grande polonaise

Paris	Conservatoire	78: Pathé PDT 270-271
1949	Orchestra	
	Darré	

John Holmes (Conductors on Record/Gollancz 1982) mentions that Cluytens conducts a recording of Chopin Piano Concerto No 2 with Marguérite Long as soloist; however, WERM/1952 lists a Columbia record of Long playing the concerto with the Conservatoire Orchestra under the conductor Gaubert

CLAUDE DEBUSSY (1862-1918)

Pelléas et Mélisande

Paris	Orchestre National	LP: HMV ALP 1522-1524
June 1956	St Paul Choir	LP: HMV (France) FALP 466-468
	De los Angeles,	LP: World Records OC 210-212
	Collard, Jansen,	CD: Testament SBT 3051
	Souzay, Froumenty	

Le martyre de Saint Sébastien, symphonic fragments

Paris   Orchestre National   LP: Columbia 33CX 1282
April 1954

La boîte à joujoux, Ballet suite arranged by Caplet

Paris   Orchestre National   LP: Columbia 33CX 1282
April-May
1954

Childrens' Corner, arranged by Caplet

Paris   Orchestre National   LP: Columbia 33CX 1282
April-May
1954

Danse sacrée et danse profane

Paris   Conservatoire   LP: Columbia 33SX 1768/SCX 3568
October 1964   Orchestra   CD: EMI CZS 568 2212
                     Challan

Fantasie pour piano et orchestre

Paris   Orchestre National   LP: International Piano Archives IPA 505
July 1955   Gieseking

Images

Paris   Conservatoire   LP: Columbia 33CX 1908/SAX 2548
1963   Orchestra   LP: World Records T 910/ST 910

Jeux

Paris   Conservatoire   LP: Columbia 33CX 1908/SAX 2548
1963   Orchestra   LP: World Records T 910/ST 910

Prélude à l'après-midi d'un faune

Moscow   Orchestre National   LP: Melodiya M10 46303 002
May 1959

MAURICE DELAGE (1879-1961)

Poèmes hindous: Madras; Lahore; Benares; Jaipore

Paris   Instrumental   78: HMV (France) DA 5054-5055
1952-1953   ensemble   45: HMV (France) 7RF 113-114
                Angelici   LP: HMV (France) FBLP 1014
                                     LP: Columbia 33CX 1353

Berceuse phoque (Chants de la jungle)

Paris   Instrumental   78: HMV (France) DA 5054-5055
1952-1953   ensemble   45: HMV (France) 7RF 113-114
                Angelici   LP: HMV (France) FBLP 1014
                                     LP: Columbia 33CX 1353

LEO DELIBES (1836-1891)

Coppélia, Ballet suite

Paris June 1956	Paris Opéra Orchestra	LP: Columbia 33CX 1505/MFP 2022 CD: Musical Note (Japan) 18MN 1006

Sylvia, Ballet suite

Paris June 1956	Paris Opéra Orchestra	LP: Columbia 33CX 1505/MFP 2022 CD: Musical Note (Japan) 18MN 1006 <u>Excerpts</u> 45: Columbia SCD 2150

PAUL DUKAS (1865-1935)

L'apprenti sorcier

Moscow May 1959	Orchestre National	LP: Melodiya M10 46303 002

ANTONIN DVORAK (1841-1904)

Symphony No 9 "From the New World", Second movement

Vienna December- January 1958	VPO	LP: HMV ALP 1736/ASD 304

MANUEL DE FALLA (1876-1946)

El sombrero de 3 picos, three dances

Paris 1949-1950	Conservatoire Orchestra	78: Pathé MDT 12-13

GABRIEL FAURE (1845-1924)

Requiem

Paris October 1950	St. Eustache Orchestra & Chorus Angelici, Noguera	LP: Columbia 33CX 1145 LP: Columbia (France) FCX 108 CD: Musical Note (Japan) 18M-1001
Paris November 1961- July 1962	Conservatoire Orchestra Brasseur Choir De los Angeles, Fischer-Dieskau	LP: EMI AN 107/SAN 107/CFP 40234 CD: EMI CDC 747 8362 Excerpt LP: EMI EX 29 04353

Ballade pour piano et orchestre

Paris April 1950	Conservatoire Orchestra Long	78: Columbia LX 8953-8954 LP: Columbia (France) FCX 169

CESAR FRANCK (1822-1890)

Symphony in D minor

Paris March 1953	Orchestre National	LP: Columbia 33CX 1064 CD: Musical Note (Japan) 18MN 1011

Variations symphoniques pour piano et orchestre

Paris June 1953	Conservatoire Orchestra Ciccolini	LP: Columbia 33CX 1190 LP: Columbia (France) FCX 30209 CD: Musical Note (Japan) 18MN 1011
Paris July 1955	Orchestre National Gieseking	CD: Hunt CDHP 588

Le chasseur maudit

Paris 1953	Conservatoire Orchestra	CD: Musical Note (Japan) 18MN 1011 LP catalogue numbers not confirmed
Brussels December 1962	Belgian National Orchestra	LP: Columbia 33CX 1884/SAX 2528 CD: EMI CDM 565 1532/CZS 568 2212

Les Djinns

Brussels December 1962	Belgian National Orchestra Ciccolini	LP: Columbia 33CX 1884/SAX 2528 CD: EMI CDM 565 1532

Les Eolides

Brussels December 1962	Belgian National Orchestra	LP: Columbia 33CX 1884/SAX 2528 CD: EMI CDM 565 1532

Psyché, 4 symphonic poems

Paris 1954-1955	Conservatoire Orchestra	CD: Musical Note (Japan) 18M-1001 <u>LP catalogue numbers not confirmed</u>

Rédemption

Paris 1953	Conservatoire Orchestra	CD: Musical Note (Japan) 18MN 1002 <u>LP catalogue number not confirmed</u>
Brussels December 1962	Belgian National Orchestra	LP: Columbia 33CX 1884/SAX 2528 CD: EMI CDM 565 1532

GEORGE GERSHWIN (1898-1937)

An American in Paris

Paris 1949-1950	Conservatoire Orchestra	78: Columbia (France) GFX 132-133

CHRISTOPH WILLIBALD GLUCK (1714-1787)

Alceste: Excerpt (Divinités du Styx!)

Paris June 1959	Paris Opéra Orchestra Gorr	LP: HMV ALP 1887/ASD 456/111 1491

Orphée et Euridice: Excerpt (J'ai perdu mon Euridice)

Paris June 1959	Paris Opéra Orchestra Gorr	LP: HMV ALP 1887/ASD 456/111 1491

CHARLES GOUNOD (1818-1893)

Faust

Paris April-May 1953	Paris Opéra Orchestra & Chorus De los Angeles, Gedda, Christoff, Borthayre	LP: HMV ALP 1162-1165/UVD 3381-3384 LP: Victor LM 6403 CD: EMI CMS 565 2562 Excerpts 45: HMV 7ER 5050/7ER 5059/7ER 5064 LP: Pathé FALPM 30151 LP: Victor LM 1825
Paris September- October 1958	Paris Opéra Orchestra & Chorus De los Angeles, Gedda, Christoff, Blanc	LP: HMV ALP 1721-1724/ASD 307-310/SLS 816 LP: Pathé CVA 630-633 LP: Angel 3622 CD: EMI CMS 769 9832 Excerpts LP: HMV ALP 1837/ASD 412 LP: Pathé CVT 3566/CVT 3567 LP: Angel 35827

Mireille

Aix-en- Provence July 1954	Conservatoire Orchestra Aix Festival Chorus Vivalda, Gedda, Dens	LP: Columbia 33CX 1299-1301 LP: EMI 2C 153 10613-10615 CD: EMI CMS 764 3822 Excerpts LP: Pathé UCD 3162 LP: Columbis (Germany) C 70411 LP: EMI 1C 137 78233-78236/SLS 5250

Mireille, Overture

Paris 1949	Opéra-Comique Orchestra	78: HMV (France) SL 138 78: HMV (Switzerland) FKX 231

JOSEF HAYDN (1732-1809)

Symphony No 94 "Surprise"

Paris 1949-1950	Conservatoire Orchestra	78: Pathé MDT 9-11

Symphony No 96 "Miracle"

Berlin September 1952	BPO	CD: Refrain (Japan) DR 92 0042

Symphony No 104 "London"

Paris 1949-1950	Conservatoire Orchestra	78: Pathé PDT 241-243

FERDINAND HEROLD (1791-1833)

La pré aux clercs, Overture

Paris 1949	Opéra-Comique Orchestra	78: Columbia (France) GFX 131

ENGLEBERT HUMPERDINCK (1854-1921)

Hänsel und Gretel

Vienna December 1963	VPO Wiener Sängerknaben Rothenberger, Seefried, Maikl, G.Hoffman, Höngen, Berry	LP: Electrola E 91366-7/STE 91366-7 LP: Angel 3648/6124 CD: EMI CMS 565 6612 Excerpts LP: EMI 1C 063 00751

VINCENT D'INDY (1851-1931)

Symphonie montagnarde pour piano et orchestre

Paris	Conservatoire	LP: Columbia 33CX 1190
June 1953	Orchestra	LP: Columbia (France) FCX 30209
	Ciccolini	CD: Musical Note (Japan) 18MN 1012

EDOUARD LALO (1823-1892)

Symphonie espagnole

Paris	Orchestra	78: Columbia (France) LFX 723-726
1948-1949	Francescatti	78: Columbia (Argentina) 500236-500239

Le roi d'Ys

Paris	Orchestre National	LP: EMI 2C 153 11068-11069
1957	and Chorus	<u>Excerpts</u>
	Micheau, Gorr,	LP: Columbia (France) FCX 30187
	Legay, Borthayre,	
	Mars	

RAOUL LAPARRA (1876-1943)

La Habanera, Act 3 Prelude

Paris	Conservatoire	78: HMV (France) W 1610
1949	Orchestra	

FRANZ LISZT (1811-1886)

Les Préludes

Berlin	BPO	Electrola unpublished
November 1960		

PIETRO MASCAGNI (1863-1945)

Cavalleria rusticana: Excerpt (Voi lo sapete)

Paris June 1959	Paris Opéra Orchestra Gorr	LP: HMV ALP 1887/ASD 456/111 1491

JULES MASSENET (1842-1912)

Werther: Excerpt (Un autre est son époux)

Paris April 1948	Opéra-Comique Orchestra Jobin	78: Columbia LX 1171 CD: EMI CHS 769 7412

Werther: Excerpt (Air des lettres)

Paris June 1959	Paris Opéra Orchestra Gorr	LP: HMV ALP 1887/ASD 456/111 1491

Phèdre, Overture

Paris October 1953	Orchestre National	CD: Musical Note (Japan) 18MN 1005 LP catalogue numbers not confirmed

Scènes alsaciennes

Paris October 1953	Orchestre National	CD: Musical Note (Japan) 18MN 1005 LP catalogue numbers not confirmed

Scènes pittoresques

Paris October 1953	Orchestre National	CD: Musical Note (Japan) 18MN 1005 LP catalogue numbers not confirmed

Les Erinnyes, incidental music to the play

Paris 1951-1952	Paris Opéra Orchestra	CD: Musical Note (Japan) 18MN 1006 LP catalogue numbers not confirmed

FELIX MENDELSSOHN-BARTHOLDY (1809-1847)

Symphony No 4 "Italian", Fourth movement

Vienna January- December 1958	VPO	45: HMV 7ER 5195/RES 4284 LP: HMV ALP 1736/ASD 304

GIAN CARLO MENOTTI (born 1911)

Piano Concerto

Paris 1954	Conservatoire Orchestra Boukoff	LP: HMV (France) FALP 176

WOLFGANG AMADEUS MOZART (1756-1791)

Symphony No 40, First movement

Vienna January- December 1958	VPO	LP: HMV ALP 1736/ASD 304

Piano Concerto No 24

Paris December 1955	Orchestre National Haskil	LP: Discocorp RR 497 CD: Disques Montaigne TCE 8780 CD: Curcio-Hunt ZAR 22 CD: Sarpe (Spain) CD 7007 CD: Music and Arts CD 863

Serenade No 13 "Eine kleine Nachtmusik", First movement

Vienna January- December 1958	VPO	45: HMV 7ER 5195/RES 4284 LP: HMV ALP 1736/ASD 304

La Clemenza di Tito: Excerpt (Se all' impero)

Paris	Conservatoire	LP: Columbia 33CX 1528
July 1957	Orchestra	LP: Angel 35510
	Gedda	LP: EMI 1C 137 78233-78236

Cosi fan tutte: Excerpt (Un aura amorosa)

Paris	Conservatoire	LP: Columbia 33CX 1528
July 1957	Orchestra	LP: Angel 35510/3204
	Gedda	LP: EMI 1C 137 78233-78236/SLS 5250

Don Giovanni, Overture

Paris	Conservatoire	78: Columbia (France) GFX 156
1955	Orchestra	

Don Giovanni: Excerpts (Dalla sua pace; Il mio tesoro)

Paris	Conservatoire	LP: Columbia 33CX 1528
July 1957	Orchestra	LP: Angel 35510
	Gedda	

Die Entführung aus dem Serail: Excerpts (O wie ängstlich; Wenn der Freude Tränen fliessen)

Paris	Conservatoire	LP: Columbia 33CX 1528
July 1957	Orchestra	LP: Angel 35510
	Gedda	

Die Entführung aus dem Serail: Excerpt (Im Mohrenland gefangen)

Paris	Conservatoire	LP: Columbia 33CX 1528
July 1957	Orchestra	LP: Angel 35510/3204
	Gedda	LP: EMI 1C 137 78233-78236/SLS 5250

Idomeneo: Excerpt (Fuor del mar)

Paris	Conservatoire	LP: Columbia 33CX 1528
July 1957	Orchestra	LP: Angel 35510
	Gedda	LP: Columbia (Germany) C 70411
		LP: EMI 1C 137 78233-78236

Die Zauberflöte: Excerpt (Dies Bildnis ist bezaubernd schön)

Paris July 1957	Conservatoire Orchestra Gedda	LP: Columbia 33CX 1528 LP: Angel 35510

Per pietà non ricercate, concert aria

Paris July 1957	Conservatoire Orchestra Gedda	LP: Columbia 33CX 1528 LP: Angel 35510 LP: EMI 1C 137 78233-78236/SLS 5250

MODEST MUSSORGSKY (1839-1881)

Boris Godunov

Paris September 1962	Conservatoire Orchestra Sofia Opera Chorus Lear, Bugarinovich, Kalin, Lanigan, Usunow, Christoff, Mars, Diakov	LP: EMI AN 110-113/SAN 110-113 LP: Angel 3633 CD: EMI CDS 747 9938 Excerpts LP: EMI ALP 2257/ASD 2257/CVT 2017

Night on Bare Mountain

Paris 1951	Conservatoire Orchestra	LP: Pathé DTX 116 LP: Vox PL 7670
London November 1958	Philharmonia	LP: Columbia 33CX 1699/SAX 2355 LP: EMI XLP 20106/SXLP 20106 CD: EMI CDM 769 1102
Moscow May 1959	Orchestre National	LP: Melodiya M10 42879-42882

Khovantschina, Prelude

Moscow May 1959	Orchestre National	LP: Melodiya M10 42879-42882

JACQUES OFFENBACH (1819-1880)

Les contes d'Hoffmann

Paris March 1948	Opéra-Comique Orchestra & Chorus Doria, Bovy, Boué, Jobin, Bourdin, Musy, Pernet	LP: Columbia 33CX 1150-1152 LP: Columbia (France) FCX 137-139 LP: Columbia (USA) SL 106 LP: EMI 2C 153 14151-14153 CD: EMI CMS 565 2602
Paris September- October 1964	Conservatoire Orchestra Duclos Choir Schwarzkopf, De los Angeles, D'Angelo, Gedda, Ghiuselev, London, Blanc	LP: EMI AN 154-156/SAN 154-156 LP: Angel 3637 LP: EMI 1C 157 00045-00047 CD: EMI CMS 763 2222 Excerpts LP: EMI ALP 2274/ASD 2274/ASD 2330 LP: EMI SXLP 30538 LP: EMI 1C 063 01967/1C 063 29044 CD: EMI CDM 763 4482/CZS 568 1132

GABRIEL PIERNE (1863-1937)

Konzertstück for harp and orchestra

Paris October 1964	Conservatoire Orchestra Challan	LP: Columbia 33SX 1768/SCX 3568 CD: EMI CZS 568 2212

FRANCIS POULENC (1899-1963)

Les mamelles de Tirésias

Paris	Opéra-Comique	LP: Columbia 33CX 1218
September 1953	Orchestra & Chorus	LP: EMI 2C 061 12510
	Duval, Giraudeau,	CD: EMI CDM 565 5622
	Jeantet, Thirache	

SERGEI PROKOFIEV (1891-1953)

Piano Concerto No 3

Paris	Conservatoire	LP: Columbia 33CX 1135
1953	Orchestra	
	François	

SERGEI RACHMANINOV (1873-1943)

Piano Concerto No 2

Paris	Conservatoire	LP: EMI XLP 20050/SXLP 20050
1962	Orchestra	LP: EMI CVD 2105/1C 053 10069
	Tacchino	

Piano Concerto No 3

Paris	Conservatoire	LP: Columbia 33CX 1323
June 1955	Orchestra	LP: EMI 1C 153 11626-11627M
	Gilels	CD: Testament SBT 1029

MAURICE RAVEL (1875-1937)

L'heure espagnole

Paris October- November 1952	Opéra-Comique Orchestra Duval, Giraudeau, Herent, Vieuille, Clavency	LP: Columbia 33CX 1076 LP: Angel 35018 CD: EMI CDM 565 2692

Alborada del gracioso

Paris June 1953	Orchestre National	45: Columbia SEL 1524 LP: Columbia 33CX 1134 CD: Musical Note (Japan) 18MN 1004
Paris November 1961- October 1962	Conservatoire Orchestra	LP: Columbia 33CX 1835/SAX 2479 LP: EMI CVB 947/CFP 40036 CD: EMI CMS 769 1652

Une barque sur l'océan

Paris November 1961- October 1962	Conservatoire Orchestra	LP: Columbia 33CX 1835/SAX 2479 LP: EMI CVB 947/CFP 40093 CD: EMI CMS 769 1652

Boléro

Paris April 1953	Orchestre National	LP: Columbia 33C 1034 CD: Musical Note (Japan) 18MN 1003
Paris November 1961- October 1962	Conservatoire Orchestra	LP: Columbia 33CX 1833/SAX 2477 LP: EMI CVB 913/CFP 40036 CD: EMI CMS 769 1652

Daphnis et Chloé, ballet

Paris November 1961- October 1962	Conservatoire Orchestra Duclos Choir	LP: Columbia 33CX 1832/SAX 2476/CVB 934 LP: World Records T 757/ST 757 <u>Published on CD in Japan</u>

Daphnis et Chloé, Suites Nos 1 and 2

Paris June 1953	Orchestre National	LP: Columbia 33CX 1134 CD: Musical Note (Japan) 18MN 1004

Introduction and Allegro

Paris October 1964	Conservatoire Orchestra Challan	LP: Columbia 33SX 1768/SCX 3568

Ma mère l'oye

Paris May 1953	Conservatoire Orchestra	78: Columbia (France) LFX 888-889 CD: Musical Note (Japan) 18MN 1003
Paris November 1961- October 1962	Conservatoire Orchestra	LP: Columbia 33CX 1834/SAX 2478/CVB 933 CD: EMI CMS 769 1652

Menuet antique

Paris May 1953	Conservatoire Orchestra	78: Columbia (France) CD: Musical Note (Japan) 18MN 1003
Paris November 1961- October 1962	Conservatoire Orchestra	LP: Columbia 33CX 1835/SAX 2479 LP: EMI CVB 947/CFP 40093 CD: EMI CMS 769 1652

Pavane pour une infante défunte

Paris May 1953	Conservatoire Orchestra	78: Pathé PDT 116 45: Columbia SEL 1524 CD: Musical Note (Japan) 18MN 1004
Paris November 1961- October 1962	Conservatoire Orchestra	LP: Columbia 33CX 1835/SAX 2479 LP: EMI CVB 947/CFP 40036 CD: EMI CMS 769 1652

Piano Concerto in G

Paris July 1959	Conservatoire Orchestra François	LP: Columbia 33CX 1747/SAX 2394/CFP 40071 LP: World Records T 871/ST 871 CD: EMI 290 4472/CDC 747 3682

Piano Concerto for the left hand

Paris July 1959	Conservatoire Orchestra François	LP: Columbia 33CX 1747/SAX 2394/CFP 40071 LP: World Records T 871/ST 871 CD: EMI 290 4472/CDC 747 3682

Rapsodie espagnole

Paris June 1953	Orchestre National	LP: Pathé DT 1005 CD: Musical Note (Japan) 18MN 1004
Moscow May 1959	Orchestre National	LP: Melodiya M10 42879-42882
Paris November 1961- October 1962	Conservatoire Orchestra	LP: Columbia 33CX 1833/SAX 2477/CVB 913 CD: EMI CMS 769 1652

Le tombeau de Couperin

Paris June 1953	Orchestre National	LP: Columbia 33C 1034 CD: Musical Note (Japan) 18MN 1003
Moscow May 1959	Orchestre National	LP: Melodiya M10 46303 002
Paris November 1961- October 1962	Conservatoire Orchestra	LP: Columbia 33CX 1835/SAX 2479 LP: EMI CVB 947/CFP 40093 CD: EMI CMS 769 1652

La valse

Paris June 1953	Orchestre National	LP: Pathé DT 1005 CD: Musical Note (Japan) 18MN 1003
London November 1958	Philharmonia	LP: Columbia 33CX 1699/SAX 2355
Paris November 1961- October 1962	Conservatoire Orchestra	LP: Columbia 33CX 1833/SAX 2477 LP: EMI CVB 913/CFP 40036 CD: EMI CMS 769 1652

Valses nobles et sentimentales

Paris June 1953	Conservatoire Orchestra	78: Columbia (France) CD: Musical Note (Japan) 18MN 1004
Paris November 1961- October 1962	Conservatoire Orchestra	LP: Columbia 33CX 1834/SAX 2478 LP: EMI CVB 933/CFP 40093 CD: EMI CMS 769 1652

NIKOLAI RIMSKY-KORSAKOV (1844-1908)

Scheherazade

Paris 1951	Orchestre National	LP: Pathé DTX 122

The Flight of the bumble bee (Tsar Saltan)

Paris September 1959	Conservatoire Orchestra	LP: Pathé CD: EMI 252 5782/CDM 769 1102

Capriccio espagnol

Paris 1951	Conservatoire Orchestra	LP: Pathé DTX 116 LP: Vox PL 7670
London November 1958	Philharmonia	LP: Columbia 33CX 1699/SAX 2355 LP: EMI XLP 20106/SXLP 20106 CD: EMI CDM 769 1102/CZS 568 0982

Russian Easter Festival Overture

Paris 1951	Conservatoire Orchestra	LP: Pathé DTX 116 LP: Vox PL 7670
Paris September 1959	Conservatoire Orchestra	LP: Pathé CD: EMI CDM 769 1102

ALBERT ROUSSEL (1869-1937)

Symphony No 3

Paris 1965	Conservatoire Orchestra	LP: Columbia CX 5251/SAX 5251

Symphony No 4

Paris 1965	Conservatoire Orchestra	LP: Columbia CX 5251/SAX 5251

Sinfonietta

Paris November 1963	Conservatoire Orchestra	LP: Columbia 33CX 1921/SAX 2562/CVB 1001 CD: EMI CZS 568 2212

Bacchus et Ariane, Suite No 2

Paris November 1963	Conservatoire Orchestra	LP: Columbia 33CX 1921/SAX 2562/CVB 1001 CD: EMI CZS 568 2212

Le festin de l'araignée

Paris November 1963	Conservatoire Orchestra	LP: Columbia 33CX 1921/SAX 2562/CVB 1001 CD: EMI CZS 568 2212

CAMILLE SAINT-SAENS (1835-1921)

Symphony No 3 "Organ"

Paris September 1955	Conservatoire Orchestra Roget	LP: Columbia 33CX 1413 CD: Musical Note (Japan) 18MN 1012

Piano Concerto No 2

Paris March 1954	Conservatoire Orchestra Gilels	LP: Columbia 33CX 1217 CD: Testament SBT 1029

La princesse jaune, Overture

Paris 1950	Conservatoire Orchestra	78: HMV (France)

Samson et Dalila: Excerpts (Printemps qui commence; Amour, viens aider ma faiblesse!)

Paris June 1959	Paris Opéra Orchestra Gorr	LP: HMV ALP 1887/ASD 456/111 1491

FRANZ SCHUBERT (1797-1828)

Symphony No 8 "Unfinished"

Paris 1951-1952	Conservatoire Orchestra	78: Columbia (France) LFX 956-958
Berlin November 1960	BPO	Electrola unpublished

ROBERT SCHUMANN (1810-1856)

Symphony No 3 "Rhenish"

Berlin   BPO   LP: HMV ALP 1779
February 1957   LP: Electrola E 70008

Symphony No 4

Paris   Orchestre National   78: Columbia (Italy) GQX 11426-11428
1952   LP: Columbia (France) FC 1001

Manfred, Overture

Berlin   BPO   LP: HMV ALP 1779
February 1957

DIMITRI SHOSTAKOVICH (1906-1975)

Symphony No 11

Paris   Orchestre National   LP: Columbia 33CX 1604-1605
May 1958   LP: Angel 3586
                                               <u>Recorded in presence of the composer</u>

Piano Concerto No 1

Paris   Orchestre National   LP: Columbia (France) FCX 769
May-September   Shostakovich   CD: EMI CDC 754 6062
1958   Vaillant, trumpet

Piano Concerto No 2

Paris   Orchestre National   LP: Columbia (France) FCX 769
May-September   Shostakovich   CD: EMI CDC 754 6062
1958

BEDRICH SMETANA (1824-1884)

The Moldau (Ma Vlast)

Vienna January 1958	VPO	LP: HMV ALP 1591 CD: Toshiba Shinseido SGR 8007

From Bohemia's Woods and Fields (Ma Vlast)

Vienna January 1958	VPO	LP: HMV ALP 1591 CD: Toshiba Shinseido SGR 8007

RICHARD STRAUSS (1864-1949)

Don Juan

Vienna January 1958	VPO	LP: HMV ALP 1591 CD: Toshiba Shinseido SGR 8007

Burleske

Paris 1948	Conservatoire Orchestra M.Meyer	78: HMV (France) W 1565-1566

Feuersnot, Love scene

Vienna January 1958	VPO	LP: HMV ALP 1591 CD: Toshiba Shinseido SGR 8007

Der Rosenkavalier: Excerpt (Di rigori armato)

Vienna May 1966	VPO Wunderlich, Edelmann, Pantscheff	Unpublished radio broadcast

IGOR STRAVINSKY (1882-1971)

L'oiseau de feu, Suite

Moscow May 1959	Orchestre National	LP: Melodiya M10 42879-42882

Perséphone

Paris January 1955	Conservatoire Orchestra and Chorus Gedda, Nollier	LP: Columbia (France) FCX 412

Le rossignol

Paris 1954	Orchestre Nationale and Chorus Micheau, Moizan, Giraudeau, Roux	LP: Columbia 33CX 1437 LP: Angel 35204
Paris 1955	Orchestre National and Chorus Micheau, Moizan, Giraudeau, Roux	CD: Disques Montaigne TCE 8760

PIOTR TCHAIKOVSKY (1840-1893)

Symphony No 4, Third movement

Vienna January- December 1958	VPO	45: HMV 7ER 5191/RES 4281 LP: HMV ALP 1736/ASD 304

Symphony No 6 "Pathétique", 3rd movement

Vienna January- December 1958	VPO	LP: HMV ALP 1736/ASD 304

Piano Concerto No 1

Paris June 1953	Conservatoire Orchestra Ciccolini	LP: HMV (France) FALP 102

GIUSEPPE VERDI (1813-1901)

Don Carlo: Excerpt (O don fatale!)

Paris June 1959	Paris Opéra Orchestra Gorr	LP: HMV ALP 1887/ASD 456/111 1491

Il Trovatore: Excerpt (Condotta all' era in ceppi)

Paris June 1959	Paris Opéra Orchestra Gorr	LP: HMV ALP 1887/ASD 456/111 1491

RICHARD WAGNER (1813-1883)

Der fliegende Holländer, Overture

Paris 1959	Paris Opéra Orchestra	LP: Pathé CVD 831 LP: EMI 3C 053 10598

Götterdämmerung, Siegfried's Rhine Journey and Funeral March

Paris 1959	Paris Opéra Orchestra	LP: Pathé Trianon 2C 045 12174

Lohengrin

Bayreuth July 1958	Bayreuth Festival Orchestra & Chorus Rysanek, Varnay, Konya, Engen, Blanc, Wächter	LP: Replica RPL 2489-2492 CD: Myto MCD 89002 <u>Excerpts</u> LP: Melodram MEL 085/MEL 590 LP: Rodolphe RP 12433-12434 CD: Melodram MEL 26101/MEL 37073

Lohengrin, Act 1 Prelude

Paris	Paris Opéra	LP: Pathé CVD 831
1959	Orchestra	LP: EMI 3C 053 10598

Lohengrin, Act 3 Prelude

Paris	Paris Opéra	LP: Pathé CVD 831
1959	Orchestra	LP: EMI 3C 053 10598
		CD: EMI 252 5782

Lohengrin: Excerpt (Entweihte Götter!)

Paris	Paris Opéra	LP: HMV ALP 1887/ASD 456/111 1491
June 1959	Orchestra	
	Gorr	

Die Meistersinger von Nürnberg

Bayreuth	Bayreuth Festival	LP: Melodram MEL 572
July 1957	Orchestra & Chorus	
	Grümmer, Milinkovic,	
	Geisler, Stolze,	
	Neidlinger, Greindl,	
	Schmitt-Walter	
Bayreuth	Bayreuth Festival	LP: Melodram MEL 582
August 1958	Orchestra & Chorus	Excerpt
	Grümmer, Schärtel,	LP: Melodram MEL 083
	Traxel, Stolze,	
	Wiener, Hotter,	
	Blankenheim	

Die Meistersinger von Nürnberg, Overture

Paris	Paris Opéra	LP: Pathé CVD 831
1959	Orchestra	LP: EMI 3C 053 10598

Parsifal

Milan 1960	La Scala Orchestra and Chorus Gorr, Caballé, Konya, Neidlinger, Christoff, Maionica	LP: Melodram MEL 437 <u>Excerpt</u> LP: Melodram MEL 658

Parsifal: Excerpt (Seit Ewigkeiten/Da traf mich sein Blick!..to end of Act 2)

Venice April 1963	La Fenice Orchestra Resnik, Thomas, Andersson	LP: Melodram MEL 667

Siegfried, Waldweben

Paris 1959	Paris Opéra Orchestra	LP: Pathé Trianon 2C 045 12174

Siegfried Idyll

Paris 1959	Paris Opéra Orchestra	LP: Pathé Trianon 2C 045 12174

Tannhäuser, Overture

Paris 1959	Paris Opéra Orchestra	LP: Pathé CVD 831 LP: EMI 3C 053 10598 CD: EMI 252 5782

Tristan und Isolde: Excerpt (Mild und leise)

Paris June 1959	Paris Opéra Orchestra Gorr	LP: HMV ALP 1887/ASD 456/111 1491

CARL MARIA VON WEBER (1786-1826)

Oberon, Overture

Paris	Opéra-Comique	78: Pathé PDT 250
1950	Orchestra	

Aufforderung zum Tanz, orchestrated by Berlioz

Paris	Conservatoire	LP: Pathé CVD 3546/2C 053 10771
September 1956	Orchestra	CD: Toshiba CC33-3739

CREDITS

Valuable help in the preparation of these discographies came from:

Yoshihiro Asada, Japan
Gary Bagnall, Co. Antrim
John Behrens, Teldec Classics Hamburg
Ray Burford, Sony Classical London
Richard Chlupaty, London
Clifford Elkin, Glasgow
Mathias Erhard, Berlin
Bill Flowers, London
Henry Fogel, Chicago
David Fulger, London
Syd Gray, Hove
Bill Holland, Warner Classics London
John T. Hughes, Orpington
Ken Jagger, EMI London
Alan Jefferson, Torpoint
Mark Kluge, Hinsdale IL
Keith Jeffrey, London
Roderick Krüsemann, Amsterdam
Ernst Lumpe, Soest
Luis Luna, Berlin
Frederick J. Maroth, Berkeley CA
Yasuo Nakanishi, Japan
Alan Newcombe, DG Hamburg
Brian Pinder, Halifax
Hans Roelofs, Antwerp
Desmond Ryall, Guildford
Alan Sanders, Richmond
Heinz Schulz, Munich
Joseph Schundelmaier, Düren
Seiichi Semba, Japan
Michael Sharman, London
Roger Smithson, London
Stewart Stehlin, New York
Neville Sumpter, Northolt
Akira Tanaka, Japan
Malcolm Walker, Harrow

Discographies by Travis & Emery:
Discographies by John Hunt.

1987: 978-1-906857-14-1: From Adam to Webern: the Recordings of von Karajan.
1991: 978-0-951026-83-0: 3 Italian Conductors and 7 Viennese Sopranos: 10 Discographies: Arturo Toscanini, Guido Cantelli, Carlo Maria Giulini, Elisabeth Schwarzkopf, Irmgard Seefried, Elisabeth Gruemmer, Sena Jurinac, Hilde Gueden, Lisa Della Casa, Rita Streich.
1992: 978-0-951026-85-4: Mid-Century Conductors and More Viennese Singers: 10 Discographies: Karl Boehm, Victor De Sabata, Hans Knappertsbusch, Tullio Serafin, Clemens Krauss, Anton Dermota, Leonie Rysanek, Eberhard Waechter, Maria Reining, Erich Kunz.
1993: 978-0-951026-87-8: More 20th Century Conductors: 7 Discographies: Eugen Jochum, Ferenc Fricsay, Carl Schuricht, Felix Weingartner, Josef Krips, Otto Klemperer, Erich Kleiber.
1994: 978-0-951026-88-5: Giants of the Keyboard: 6 Discographies: Wilhelm Kempff, Walter Gieseking, Edwin Fischer, Clara Haskil, Wilhelm Backhaus, Artur Schnabel.
1994: 978-0-951026-89-2: Six Wagnerian Sopranos: 6 Discographies: Frieda Leider, Kirsten Flagstad, Astrid Varnay, Martha Moedl, Birgit Nilsson, Gwyneth Jones.
1995: 978-0-952582-70-0: Musical Knights: 6 Discographies: Henry Wood, Thomas Beecham, Adrian Boult, John Barbirolli, Reginald Goodall, Malcolm Sargent.
1995: 978-0-952582-71-7: A Notable Quartet: 4 Discographies: Gundula Janowitz, Christa Ludwig, Nicolai Gedda, Dietrich Fischer-Dieskau.
1996: 978-0-952582-72-4: The Post-War German Tradition: 5 Discographies: Rudolf Kempe, Joseph Keilberth, Wolfgang Sawallisch, Rafael Kubelik, Andre Cluytens.
1996: 978-0-952582-73-1: Teachers and Pupils: 7 Discographies: Elisabeth Schwarzkopf, Maria Ivoguen, Maria Cebotari, Meta Seinemeyer, Ljuba Welitsch, Rita Streich, Erna Berger.
1996: 978-0-952582-77-9: Tenors in a Lyric Tradition: 3 Discographies: Peter Anders, Walther Ludwig, Fritz Wunderlich.
1997: 978-0-952582-78-6: The Lyric Baritone: 5 Discographies: Hans Reinmar, Gerhard Huesch, Josef Metternich, Hermann Uhde, Eberhard Waechter.
1997: 978-0-952582-79-3: Hungarians in Exile: 3 Discographies: Fritz Reiner, Antal Dorati, George Szell.
1997: 978-1-901395-00-6: The Art of the Diva: 3 Discographies: Claudia Muzio, Maria Callas, Magda Olivero.
1997: 978-1-901395-01-3: Metropolitan Sopranos: 4 Discographies: Rosa Ponselle, Eleanor Steber, Zinka Milanov, Leontyne Price.
1997: 978-1-901395-02-0: Back From The Shadows: 4 Discographies: Willem Mengelberg, Dimitri Mitropoulos, Hermann Abendroth, Eduard Van Beinum.
1997: 978-1-901395-03-7: More Musical Knights: 4 Discographies: Hamilton Harty, Charles Mackerras, Simon Rattle, John Pritchard.
1998: 978-1-901395-94-5: Conductors On The Yellow Label: 8 Discographies: Fritz Lehmann, Ferdinand Leitner, Ferenc Fricsay, Eugen Jochum, Leopold Ludwig, Artur Rother, Franz Konwitschny, Igor Markevitch.
1998: 978-1-901395-95-2: More Giants of the Keyboard: 5 Discographies: Claudio Arrau, Gyorgy Cziffra, Vladimir Horowitz, Dinu Lipatti, Artur Rubinstein.
1998: 978-1-901395-96-9: Mezzo and Contraltos: 5 Discographies: Janet Baker, Margarete Klose, Kathleen Ferrier, Giulietta Simionato, Elisabeth Hoengen.

1999: 978-1-901395-97-6: The Furtwaengler Sound Sixth Edition: Discography and Concert Listing.
1999: 978-1-901395-98-3: The Great Dictators: 3 Discographies: Evgeny Mravinsky, Artur Rodzinski, Sergiu Celibidache.
1999: 978-1-901395-99-0: Sviatoslav Richter: Pianist of the Century: Discography.
2000: 978-1-901395-04-4: Philharmonic Autocrat 1: Discography of: Herbert Von Karajan [Third Edition].
2000: 978-1-901395-05-1: Wiener Philharmoniker 1 - Vienna Philharmonic and Vienna State Opera Orchestras: Discography Part 1 1905-1954.
2000: 978-1-901395-06-8: Wiener Philharmoniker 2 - Vienna Philharmonic and Vienna State Opera Orchestras: Discography Part 2 1954-1989.
2001: 978-1-901395-07-5: Gramophone Stalwarts: 3 Separate Discographies: Bruno Walter, Erich Leinsdorf, Georg Solti.
2001: 978-1-901395-08-2: Singers of the Third Reich: 5 Discographies: Helge Roswaenge, Tiana Lemnitz, Franz Voelker, Maria Mueller, Max Lorenz.
2001: 978-1-901395-09-9: Philharmonic Autocrat 2: Concert Register of Herbert Von Karajan Second Edition.
2002: 978-1-901395-10-5: Sächsische Staatskapelle Dresden: Complete Discography.
2002: 978-1-901395-11-2: Carlo Maria Giulini: Discography and Concert Register.
2002: 978-1-901395-12-9: Pianists For The Connoisseur: 6 Discographies: Arturo Benedetti Michelangeli, Alfred Cortot, Alexis Weissenberg, Clifford Curzon, Solomon, Elly Ney.
2003: 978-1-901395-14-3: Singers on the Yellow Label: 7 Discographies: Maria Stader, Elfriede Troetschel, Annelies Kupper, Wolfgang Windgassen, Ernst Haefliger, Josef Greindl, Kim Borg.
2003: 978-1-901395-15-0: A Gallic Trio: 3 Discographies: Charles Muench, Paul Paray, Pierre Monteux.
2004: 978-1-901395-16-7: Antal Dorati 1906-1988: Discography and Concert Register.
2004: 978-1-901395-17-4: Columbia 33CX Label Discography.
2004: 978-1-901395-18-1: Great Violinists: 3 Discographies: David Oistrakh, Wolfgang Schneiderhan, Arthur Grumiaux.
2006: 978-1-901395-19-8: Leopold Stokowski: Second Edition of the Discography.
2006: 978-1-901395-20-4: Wagner Im Festspielhaus: Discography of the Bayreuth Festival.
2006: 978-1-901395-21-1: Her Master's Voice: Concert Register and Discography of Dame Elisabeth Schwarzkopf [Third Edition].
2007: 978-1-901395-22-8: Hans Knappertsbusch: Kna: Concert Register and Discography of Hans Knappertsbusch, 1888-1965. Second Edition.
2008: 978-1-901395-23-5: Philips Minigroove: Second Extended Version of the European Discography.
2009: 978-1-901395--24-2: American Classics: The Discographies of Leonard Bernstein and Eugene Ormandy.

Discography by Stephen J. Pettitt, edited by John Hunt:
1987: 978-1-906857-16-5: Philharmonia Orchestra: Complete Discography 1945-1987

Available from: Travis & Emery at 17 Cecil Court, London, UK. (+44) 20 7 240 2129. email on sales@travis-and-emery.com .

© Travis & Emery 2009

Music and Books published by Travis & Emery Music Bookshop:
Anon.: Hymnarium Sarisburiense, cum Rubricis et Notis Musicis.
Agricola, Johann Friedrich from Tosi: Anleitung zur Singkunst.
Bach, C.P.E.: edited W. Emery: Nekrolog or Obituary Notice of J.S. Bach.
Bateson, Naomi Judith: Alcock of Salisbury
Bathe, William: A Briefe Introduction to the Skill of Song
Bax, Arnold: Symphony #5, Arranged for Piano Four Hands by Walter Emery
Burney, Charles: The Present State of Music in France and Italy
Burney, Charles: The Present State of Music in Germany, The Netherlands ...
Burney, Charles: An Account of the Musical Performances ... Handel
Burney, Karl: Nachricht von Georg Friedrich Handel's Lebensumstanden.
Cobbett, W.W.: Cobbett's Cyclopedic Survey of Chamber Music. (2 vols.)
Corrette, Michel: Le Maitre de Clavecin
Crimp, Bryan: Dear Mr. Rosenthal ... Dear Mr. Gaisberg ...
Crimp, Bryan: Solo: The Biography of Solomon
d'Indy, Vincent: Beethoven: Biographie Critique
d'Indy, Vincent: Beethoven: A Critical Biography
d'Indy, Vincent: César Franck (in French)
Frescobaldi, Girolamo: D'Arie Musicali per Cantarsi. Primo & Secondo Libro.
Geminiani, Francesco: The Art of Playing the Violin.
Handel; Purcell; Boyce; Geene et al: Calliope or English Harmony: Volume First.
Hawkins, John: A General History of the Science and Practice of Music (5 vols.)
Herbert-Caesari, Edgar: The Science and Sensations of Vocal Tone
Herbert-Caesari, Edgar: Vocal Truth
Hopkins and Rimboult: The Organ. Its History and Construction.
Hunt, John: Adam to Webern: the recordings of von Karajan
Isaacs, Lewis: Hänsel and Gretel. A Guide to Humperdinck's Opera.
Isaacs, Lewis: Königskinder (Royal Children) A Guide to Humperdinck's Opera.
Lacassagne, M. l'Abbé Joseph : Traité Général des élémens du Chant.
Lascelles (née Catley), Anne: The Life of Miss Anne Catley.
Mainwaring, John: Memoirs of the Life of the Late George Frederic Handel
Malcolm, Alexander: A Treaty of Music: Speculative, Practical and Historical
Marx, Adolph Bernhard: Die Kunst des Gesanges, Theoretisch-Practisch
May, Florence: The Life of Brahms
Mellers, Wilfrid: Angels of the Night: Popular Female Singers of Our Time
Mellers, Wilfrid: Bach and the Dance of God
Mellers, Wilfrid: Beethoven and the Voice of God

Travis & Emery Music Bookshop
17 Cecil Court, London, WC2N 4EZ, United Kingdom.
Tel. (+44) 20 7240 2129

Music and Books published by Travis & Emery Music Bookshop:
Mellers, Wilfrid: Caliban Reborn - Renewal in Twentieth Century Music
Mellers, Wilfrid: François Couperin and the French Classical Tradition
Mellers, Wilfrid: Harmonious Meeting
Mellers, Wilfrid: Le Jardin Retrouvé, The Music of Frederic Mompou
Mellers, Wilfrid: Music and Society, England and the European Tradition
Mellers, Wilfrid: Music in a New Found Land: ... ... American Music
Mellers, Wilfrid: Romanticism and the Twentieth Century (from 1800)
Mellers, Wilfrid: The Masks of Orpheus: ...... the Story of European Music.
Mellers, Wilfrid: The Sonata Principle (from c. 1750)
Mellers, Wilfrid: Vaughan Williams and the Vision of Albion
Panchianio, Cattuffio: Rutzvanscad Il Giovine
Pearce, Charles: Sims Reeves, Fifty Years of Music in England.
Playford, John: An Introduction to the Skill of Musick.
Purcell, Henry et al: Harmonia Sacra ... The First Book, (1726)
Purcell, Henry et al: Harmonia Sacra ... Book II (1726)
Quantz, Johann: Versuch einer Anweisung die Flöte traversiere zu spielen.
Rameau, Jean-Philippe: Code de Musique Pratique, ou Methodes.
Rastall, Richard: The Notation of Western Music.
Rimbault, Edward: The Pianoforte, Its Origins, Progress, and Construction.
Rousseau, Jean Jacques: Dictionnaire de Musique
Rubinstein, Anton : Guide to the proper use of the Pianoforte Pedals.
Sainsbury, John S.: Dictionary of Musicians. Vol. 1. (1825). 2 vols.
Simpson, Christopher: A Compendium of Practical Musick in Five Parts
Spohr, Louis: Autobiography
Spohr, Louis: Grand Violin School
Tans'ur, William: A New Musical Grammar; or The Harmonical Spectator
Terry, Charles Sanford: Four-Part Chorals of J.S. Bach. (German & English)
Terry, Charles Sanford: Joh. Seb. Bach, Cantata Texts, Sacred and Secular.
Terry, Charles Sanford: The Origins of the Family of Bach Musicians.
Tosi, Pierfrancesco: Opinioni de' Cantori Antichi, e Moderni
Van der Straeten, Edmund: History of the Violoncello, The Viol da Gamba ...
Van der Straeten, Edmund: History of the Violin, Its Ancestors... (2 vols.)
Walther, J. G.: Musicalisches Lexikon ober Musicalische Bibliothec

Travis & Emery Music Bookshop
17 Cecil Court, London, WC2N 4EZ, United Kingdom.
Tel. (+44) 20 7240 2129
© Travis & Emery 2009

www.ingramcontent.com/pod-product-compliance
Lightning Source LLC
Chambersburg PA
CBHW070940230426
43666CB00011B/2511